Leading at the
Speed of Light

Issues in Twenty-First Century Warfare

Leading at the Speed of Light

New Strategies for U.S. Security in the Information Age

DANIEL M. GERSTEIN

Potomac Books, Inc.
Washington, D.C.

Library of Congress Cataloging-in-Publication Data

Gerstein, Daniel M., 1958-
Leading at the speed of light : new strategies for U.S. security in the information age / Daniel M. Gerstein. — 1st ed.
p. cm.
Includes bibliographical references and index.

1. National security—United States. 2. Information systems—Protection—United States. 3. Cyberterrorism—United States—Prevention. 4. Political leadership—United States. I. Title.
UA23.G552 2006
355'.033573—dc22
2006023380

Hardcover ISBN-10: 1-59797-059-X
Hardcover ISBN-13: 978-1-59797-059-4

Softcover ISBN-10: 1-59797-060-3
Softcover ISBN-13: 978-1-59797-060-0

(alk. paper)

Printed in Canada on acid-free paper that meets the American National Standards Institute Z39-48 Standard.

Potomac Books, Inc.
22841 Quicksilver Drive
Dulles, Virginia 20166

First Edition

10 9 8 7 6 5 4 3 2 1

For Kathy, Sarah, and Rachel …

Contents

Tables and Figures

Tables

Figures

Preface

This is an important time in America's history. America is a super power in every sense of the word; some have even used the term "hyperpower" to describe America's role in the world. But America, and indeed much of the world, is moving into the Information Age at a staggering rate. The question before us today is, are American leaders capable of and willing to respond to this challenge and develop the structures, organizations, and insights to continue as the single most dominant nation on the face of the planet? More pointedly, will the American empire survive? Whole volumes have been written to debate this question. My purpose is not to address this empire issue, but rather the question of how leaders and leadership must change in this new environment.

Many today see terrorism or extremism as the major issue facing the United States. Since 9/11, the United States has been waging war in distant lands: Afghanistan, Iraq, and the Philippines are a few countries where American military force or hard power has been applied. This war has also been waged across virtually every corner of the globe using political, legal, and intelligence resources. The original Global War on Terror (GWOT) has been replaced by the global war on extremism, but the goals remain the same: to find, kill, or capture terrorists and extremists before they can act to threaten U.S. interests, either at home or abroad.

Some point to the rise of China as the major threat to the United States in the future. A Department of Defense (DoD) report published in May 2006 details the military buildup that is underway in China, including developing power projection capabilities with global reach.[1] Certainly China has undertaken a long-term effort to build economic power, compete as a leader on the world's stage, and even develop military capabilities that rival or at least match those of the United States.

Still others see international organizations such as the United Nations as a threat, potentially diffusing U.S. power and leading to a global group think. They see a homogenization in which America is forced to compromise and cooperate in ways that are sometimes less than optimal for our security and defense for the greater good of the other nations. People in this category fear the impact of multilateralism on U.S. national security.

Perhaps there are some that see no major threat to American dominance on the world scene, although this group surely would be in the minority given events in New York, London, and Madrid since 2001.

The Department of Defense has identified four future challenges the United States is expected to face:[2]

1. Traditional. Those seeking to challenge American power by instigating traditional military operations with legacy and advanced military capabilities. Examples include conventional, air, land, and sea forces and nuclear forces of established nuclear powers.
2. Irregular. Those seeking to erode American influence and power by employing unconventional or irregular methods. Examples include terrorism, insurgency, civil war, and emerging concepts such as "unrestricted war."
3. Disruptive. Those seeking to usurp American power and influence by acquiring breakthrough capabilities. Examples include sensors, information, biotechnology, and miniaturization on the molecular level, cyber-operations, space, directed energy, and other emerging technologies.
4. Catastrophic. Those seeking to paralyze American leadership and power by employing weapons of mass destruction (WMD) or WMD-like effects in unwarned attacks on symbolic, critical, or other high value targets. Examples include 9/11, terrorist use of WMD, or rogue missile attack.

While not disagreeing with the characterization of the four future challenges, I do argue that the major threats facing the United States today result not simply from terrorists, groups, or even countries, but rather from adverse reactions to the Information Age fueled by technologies that have changed the global relationships to which we have grown accustomed. This globalization has brought societies together while fracturing others, made the world more interconnected, allowed windows into places that were once remote and distant but now come into our lives with increasing regularity, made borders more porous, increased productivity, and served as a medium for transnational networks with both peaceful and nefarious purposes. In short, globalization has changed the very time, distance, and ideological relationships of the past. The number of threats and challenges has grown and will continue to increase with the continued proliferation of information technologies and the inherent globalization. Regardless of whether one is a great power "junkie" who sees China as the major strategic threat, or a counterterrorism proponent who sees the civilized world in a great battle between good and evil, the fuel that will ignite and sustain these future challenges is globalization propelled by the spread of information technologies.

But the news is not all bad. Along with a growth in the challenges facing America, there will also be unprecedented opportunities for increasing productivity, learning more about our planet and galaxy, providing higher standards of living and longer life spans, and decreasing human suffering.

The balance between challenges and opportunity rests squarely on the leaders and leadership of the United States. This includes national, state, and local leaders having the understanding of this new era, and the will and courage to act on the new demands of the Information Age. Consider a few examples where we have to date allowed opportunities to be squandered.

Today our government suffers from gridlock and inefficiencies as a result of partisan political battles that divert attention from the real security issues facing America. Political nominations are held up because Congress wants additional information on a leasing deal for air force tanker fleet modernization. Many nominated to fill key openings within the government are simply not qualified. Consider Michael Brown, the director of the Federal Emergency Management Agency (FEMA), who resigned on September 12, 2005, in the aftermath of a poor personal and organizational performance after Hurricane Katrina. Judgeships sit idle, awaiting confirmation of "unconfirmable" judges. Positions within the security apparatus of the United States are vacant or filled by individuals serving as "acting" secretaries. If we are really in a war, would we not want to have the ranks filled in DoD? We certainly would not send a unit to battle without its top leaders, why should it be acceptable at the department level? Consider the post-9/11 debates about intelligence reforms and the structure of Homeland Security. Which agencies are responsible or share the blame is not relevant. Regardless of who is responsible, there are real issues involving security and defense not being addressed either because key positions in DoD were unfilled, because the focus was elsewhere, or because of bureaucratic infighting.

Another example concerns the lack of a national system of identification. Why is there no national identification card system in place? Is this a matter of states' rights or individual liberties? A national ID card could contain biometric data and other critical information that would allow access to a variety of venues, including mass transportation, shopping malls, and national parks across the country. Those individuals having the ID cards, thereby submitting to some invasion of privacy, would be rewarded with immediate access; those not participating could still gain access but would need to go through additional checks and further scrutiny. Certainly with the appropriate level of leadership, we could solve these issues and better protect America.

America continues to fixate on 9/11, dedicating vast resources to try to stop another attack executed in this exact manner; certainly we must continue to guard the airline system as it remains vulnerable, as the foiled plot to explode multiple airliners over the Atlantic Ocean in August 2006 highlights. However, there is also a high probability of a different kind of attack on our infrastructure. What must be done to secure the rest of the national transportation system, safeguard our ports and borders, protect key industrial areas, and halt the proliferation of threatening technologies? This is even more important when one considers that approximately 85 percent of the critical infrastructure in our country is privately held. To be fair, much progress has been made since 9/11 and American society is much more aware of these issues than it was prior to the attacks, but when we start from the bottom as we did post-9/11, there is a long way to go.

We are in a race against time between the terrorists that threaten America and our ability to protect our nation through active and passive measures.

The problem is even more acute at the state and local levels. The national system with the Department of Homeland Security (DHS) has been established and even tested and exercised. The military effort that supports this department, Northern Command (NORTHCOM), has established support capabilities to assist in various activities such as detection and support during and immediately following an attack. These exercises include the states with the involvement of governors and their response forces. Despite the efforts of federal and even many state governments, not enough exercises have been conducted to ensure that local leaders are prepared for the responses that would be required. The issue of response is exacerbated by the commitment of the National Guard to combat operations in Iraq and Afghanistan; many of these response forces are no longer available to state leaders. The problem becomes more acute at the local level, where local community leaders—including nongovernmental business leaders—are largely left on their own to procure the necessary capabilities for protection against and mitigation of any potential attack. Unfortunately the results to date have been mixed.

The response to Hurricane Katrina, which has received much warranted as well as undeserved critisism, provides an illustration of how the logjams can be broken and creative and adaptive leadership and planning can result in a much-improved response to a regional or national tragedy. In a span of less than twenty-four hours, assets from across the nation were mobilized and reported to the Department of Homeland Security in deployed locations at the disaster area to provide critical responses. Over fifteen government agencies or departments reported in with capabilities to alleviate the immediate situation and begin planning for the longer-range reconstruction of the Gulf Coast. There were significant missteps and confusion along the way, but one can only imagine how much more challenging the effort would have been pre-9/11, before the special consequence management procedures and capabilities had been put in place and exercised on a routine basis. But even this response lacked the magnitude necessary for a major manmade or natural disaster. More can and must be done to secure America from the various threats in the world.

Pictures of parking lots full of buses flooded before they were used to evacuate citizens illustrate how local leaders remain unprepared or unwilling to act with appropriate speed and purpose.

For each of these examples, twenty-first-century leadership and leaders of vision will be the key. As a nation we must rise above partisan politics, fears of governmental interference, and fighting the last battle to arrive at timely and innovative solutions to the security and defense issues facing the country.

The reader may question why a book on leadership is focusing on one narrowly oriented group of leaders, those involved in the development and execution of national security strategy and policy. First, little has been discussed or written about the impact of globalization and proliferation of information technology on the leader. While the expansion of capabilities and information technologies is largely driven by science and engineering and can be measured, the impact on the human dimension and leaders in particular is not nearly as easily measured or understood. I therefore believe it is time to look at the human dimension in this area.

Additionally, I have spent my entire adult life, some thirty years thinking about, debating, and practicing national security as an army officer. This is my field of expertise and the field in which I have had the opportunity to observe and catalog my experiences and those of the leaders in the field of security and defense of our nation, both military and civilian alike. For this reason, I have chosen to focus most closely on leadership in national security, although I hope that my observations and conclusions will have broader application to leaders beyond this specific field.

Finally, I believe that this book addresses a seam between two interrelated subjects, national security strategy and leadership. In my research for a previous book titled *Securing America's Future: National Strategy in the Information Age*, which dealt with the impact of globalization on national security strategy, I became convinced that our nation's security strategy, and indeed the organization and structures of national security, needed to adapt to the changes in the global environment to better reflect and account for the realities of this new era. In the latter sections of *Securing America's Future*, I examined some of the requisite changes to implement in the field of leadership in an overview fashion. However, I believe that the relationship between a new national security strategy and leadership demands more focus and thus the idea for a book dedicated to this topic was developed.

This project does not claim to be the definitive work on leadership, nor does it cover all the different leadership theories and concepts. Certainly these topics will be addressed as they assist in the understanding of the relationship between national security and strategy. One should also not expect to be able to use this book as a sole-source leadership text that will lead to an instantaneous transformation in one's leadership skills. Rather the attempt is to take the body of knowledge concerning classic leadership and develop conclusions concerning how the Information Age will impact leadership requirements for national security leaders in this new age.

Additionally, this book does not address a topic closely related but distinct from leadership, that of management. In *Military Leadership* by Robert Taylor and William Rosenbach, the editors call leadership and management "two distinct but complementary systems,"[3] and make the distinction: "Many people define management as a set of functions—planning, organizing and controlling—that can be taught and learned. Leadership is an influence process. The end result is evaluation in terms of unit or organizational objective."[4]

In *Leading at the Speed of Light*, some of the management functions certainly overlap and are thus attributed to leadership. Given that functions such as planning, organizing, and controlling lead to the accomplishment of organizational objectives, and that management and leadership are complementary, it seems reasonable that some discussion of these management functions would naturally surface in a book on leadership.

My personal interest in leadership began with my early studies as a cadet at the United States Military Academy at West Point. Over the course of the four-year curriculum, there were many opportunities to discuss leaders and their organizations. Theories abound about what makes a leader or organization successful. Some theories focus on born leadership, others on learned behavior. From my perspective, the debate continued for my four years with little solid evidence as to which camp was right. In my mind, the debate continues today, with no definitive outcome.

Throughout my military education, I have found myself drawn to the study of leaders and leadership within the broader subject of history. Many times, we would examine and deconstruct an event in history and determine a cause and effect relationship for why leaders, units, and organizations either succeeded or failed. For me, history seemed to contain many examples of leaders that were both successful and unsuccessful.

But this study also raised additional questions. How does one explain successful leaders that rise to the pinnacle of their professions only to suffer a humiliating defeat at a crucial point? These great captains then take on the mantle of failure. Did they really go from great leaders to humiliated losers in an instant? Or was there something else that helped to determine their destinies?

During my military service, I watched leaders at the lowest and highest levels of the organization to see if there were any particular traits that could give a hint as to how well organizations fared. Clearly there were some common characteristics of the leaders that I sought to emulate, but there did not appear to be a map that translated leadership traits into successful organizations. In fact, in some cases, I saw leaders that I admired commanding organizations that were not particularly successful outfits.

So what makes the leader successful? Is it how well the organization performs? Is it related to how well the leader is liked or respected within an organization? Is it the teaching, coaching, and mentoring that the leader does to prepare tomorrow's leaders, sometimes known as building the bench? These topics will be my focus with the added investigation into how leaders and leadership will need to evolve to the changes in the environment resultant from the globalization in the Information Age.

Acknowledgments

Leadership is a highly personal and subjective discipline. It springs from the heart of the leader and truly represents the many experiences of the individual both as a subordinate and in the leadership roles that he or she has held. As such, leaders are all an amalgamation of their various experiences. In one sense they are trapped by their pasts, while in another, they are enabled by these experiences.

Looking at myself, I see traits of all of the leaders and mentors I have had throughout a military career that has spanned almost thirty years. I see pieces (albeit small pieces) of the "natural" leaders that I have encountered that seem to ease into the leadership role effortlessly. They can lead from the front or the rear. Position makes no difference; rather, the ability to lead is what sets them apart. I also see pieces in myself of those leaders that exercise authority using more of the elements of control rather than command. They analyze in great detail every aspect of a situation prior to making leadership decisions. Others are all about command and know little or nothing of control. I have also been fortunate to witness some truly brilliant thinkers whose reasoning and understanding give insights that few are able to master; even some of this periodically emerges in me. In these leaders, subordinates can sense these abilities, and they follow out of confidence and respect. And of course, there are the mission-first types who always get the job done at any cost. Sometimes I catch a glimpse of this type of leader in myself as well.

In this quest to understand leadership, I also see many subordinates I have been fortunate to lead. It is really the subordinates who give the leader power. And so we must recognize the preeminent role of the individual as part of a larger organization or military formation.

I also see my peers, beginning in the formative years at West Point as we developed and refined our leadership skills on each other—sometimes a painful process, but certainly a necessary one—and the many colleagues during my time in various commands or on staffs. Each provided important input for my personal development as a leader.

Therefore, I owe this book to the leaders, peers, and subordinates who have helped to form me. I have never considered myself a purely natural leader, nor do I see myself as a brilliant strategist or communicator. But I do believe that over the course of my military service, I have developed certain leadership characteristics and traits that reflect my many experiences. I also believe that both as a leader and a human being I am better for these interactions.

The development and writing of this book is also due in large measure to a selective group of leaders, mentors, peers, and subordinates that have caused me to think outside the box and to examine the future through different lenses. I have been allowed and even encouraged to look at problems and issues in a strategic sense and with a long-term perspective. Many times people with mutual interests in thinking critically about the future, regardless of rank, came together to discuss their views of the future of warfare, the emerging changes in international relations, or leadership. Despite the reputation of the military as being regimented and not allowing much creativity, I have always found the opposite to be true. This book is really an offshoot of this creative thinking.

The idea for this book began on a weekend during my brigade command tour as I thought about how to explain to my junior leaders the importance of developing a vision for their units and being able to communicate that vision down to the lowest levels of their respective organizations. When I shared these ideas with these junior officers, a dialogue occurred, during which their feedback and excitement generated new ideas for this book.

This book also stems from the realization that changes are occurring around the world based on globalization that will forever alter the relationships between nations and peoples. Thus the importance of well-articulated U.S. leadership to navigate the turbulent twenty-first century will be imperative to secure America's future.

CHAPTER 1

Strategy and Leadership

In *Securing America's Future: National Strategy in the Information Age*, I discussed the impact of globalization on our national security and its subsequent impact on the development of the grand strategy for the United States in the twenty-first century. The thesis was that as the world moved into the Information Age at a rapid pace, success in this new environment demanded a different approach to national security and strategy. The book described a set of principles for the Information Age that mandated innovative approaches to the development of national security strategy. The case was made for broader application and employment of the elements of national power. For too long, the United States has depended on the hard power elements—political, military, and intelligence—while failing to appropriately make use of what have become known as the soft power capabilities including such elements of national power as economics, education, human rights, media and public diplomacy, health, science and technology, and the environment.

In this book a similar case is made. If a globalized and highly interconnected world, linked by information technology with data traveling at light speeds along the World Wide Web, impacts the development of national security strategy, then it follows that the practitioner of a new twenty-first-century strategy for the United States must undergo a corresponding change. More directly, the Information Age defender of the United States must have a different and perhaps expanded set of skills, capabilities, and experiences to be able to successfully apply the strategies that have been developed. But what changes are required in leadership and how can these changes occur?

Despite all the technological changes over the course of human history, the development of the human mind has not progressed on the same scale. We have gone from travel by foot to space travel, but the human mind "operates" or "computes" in much the same way it has since the emergence of modern humans. Certainly the body of knowledge to which the average human has access has increased dramatically, but the human way in which inputs are perceived, cataloged, and analyzed has not changed.

A second, equally important point made in *Securing America's Future* was the need for the national security strategist to think differently about strategy development in the twenty-first century. The complexity of the Information Age environment requires greater expertise across a broader range of disciplines and places far greater demands on the strategist. To account for these increased requirements, the formulation of strategy must be changed accordingly. Whereas previously, strategy has been defined as the linking of *ways* and *mean*s to achieve *ends* while mitigating *risk*, the case was made to include the *environment* into future discussions of strategy. In this construct, the *ways* and *means* represent the processes and the resources of the strategy, respectively. The goals or objectives are captured in the *ends*. Incorporating *risk* into the formulation of strategy reflects the understanding that the outcome of any strategy dependent on friction or "fog of war" as a way to address the potential range of outcomes possible from the combining of *ways* and *means*. Finally, the incorporation of the *environment* addresses the external forces and the actors on which the strategy is applied. Without addressing this factor, a strategy will reflect a very one-sided formulation where *ends*, *ways*, *means*, and *risk* are all identified from the perspective of the strategist developing the plan. Only the *environment* accounts for the perspective of the actor or actors on which the strategy is being exercised.

The information revolution and the accompanying globalization reflect a significant change in the strategic *environment* that cannot be overlooked. The Information Age will result in a natural amalgamation of peoples across the globe, and with this mixing of societies will come the potential for a fracturing of nations and societies. The first phenomenon is called globalization, defined as:

> the emergence of a global society in which economic, political, environmental, and cultural events in one part of the world quickly come to have significance for people in other parts of the world. Globalization is the result of advances in communication, transportation, and information technologies.[1]

The second force is called irredentism, an equally powerful force driving nations, societies, and peoples apart by fueling the frictions and tensions of societies brought closer together through the use of information technologies.

Changes resulting from globalization will also allow for the proliferation of, as well as a pure growth in, *means* available. Whereas previously the hard power elements were the primary tools of strategy, now the soft power elements must also be factored in the strategy equation. Just examining the military element of power provides ample evidence of the growth of means. Consider the progression of armaments from swords, pikes, spears, and arrows used by militaries in Napoleonic warfare in contrast to tanks, aircraft, nuclear weapons, satellites, and submarines used today. With the proliferation of advanced systems, the reach available to combatants has continued to grow dramatically as well. As an example, consider that the average number of soldiers deployed per square kilometer of front has declined drastically: 3,883 during the U.S. Civil War, 404 in World War I, 36 in World War II, 25 in the 1973 Yom Kippur War, and 2 in the 1991 Gulf War.[2] This discussion has not even begun to address the potential of the Information Age that will be inherent by overlaying a network on top of today's battle systems to allow for interoperability and eventually interdependence among systems within the battlespace. The result will be the ability to attack virtually anywhere on the globe from distances halfway around the world.

The Information Age has also facilitated the growth of whole new areas of technology. For example, today we are seeing the early stages of capabilities for attacking computer networks from vast distances and nanotechnology that combines biology and computers. These advances will certainly increase the means available to potential adversaries. In fact, a whole new category of operation has merged relating to information operations (IO). In response, the military has subdivided IO into several core elements including operations security (OPSEC), psychological operations (PSYOP), military deception (MD), electronic warfare (EW), and computer network operations (CNO), which is further divided into computer network attack, defense, and exploitation (CNA, CND, and CNE).[3] The component terms alone provide ample demonstration of the complexity of this new field related to information technology and globalization. Each of the elements concentrates on a different aspect of IO, such as protection of friendly information as in the case of OPSEC and CND. Others, such as PSYOP and MD, work to influence foreign decision makers and peoples while still others are intended to defend the electromagnetic spectrum, such as EW. The point is not to become expert in each of these core elements, but rather to understand that new types of warfare and defensive measures have been created as a result of the information explosion.

The issue becomes more complex with the emergence of dual use technologies, which have application in civil society as well as potential use as weapons, such as nuclear, biological, and chemical technologies that can be used to develop weapons of mass destruction. The same technology used to build a nuclear power plant has application in the field of nuclear bomb development. The same is true for biotechnology, which has great potential to eliminate and control diseases such as smallpox, but can also be weaponized to the detriment of global society. The analogy continues for chemical technologies, where chemicals such as those used in fertilizers are very similar to chemical weapons that can be used with great effect on the battlefield or against populations, as evidenced by the massive number of gas casualties in World War I and by Saddam Hussein in the 1990s against the Kurds in northern Iraq. The attacks of 9/11 demonstrate that even systems developed solely for civilian purposes can serve as crude but effective weapons of mass destruction.

The previous discussion demonstrates how systems can be brought together in combinations or separately to achieve strategic outcomes. Over time, the development of new methodologies, capabilities, and doctrine have allowed for an almost limitless set of *ways* in which strategic interactions can occur. Whereas strategy previously was limited to the political-military-intelligence applications of hard power on the field of battle, today the battlespace has been expanded to the point where computer hackers can wage war from thousands of miles away using relatively low-cost, commercially available systems to great effect.

The *ways* and *means* are certainly not the only components of strategy that have evolved. Even the *ends* of our national strategy as expressed by the commitment of forces abroad have changed dramatically throughout our history.[4] The frequency of operations, the types of operations, and the stated *ends* for the employment of the military element of national power have been broadened to reflect the goals of the United States.

In the one-hundred-year period from 1798 to 1898, the United States employed armed forces abroad in ninety-eight cases. Analysis indicates that each of these deployments of force were for one of four narrowly defined and relatively short duration purposes: (1) to protect American lives and property or punish others for indiscretions against American citizens or property, (2) ensure freedom of navigation, (3) acquire additional lands, or (4) protect the territorial integrity of the United States. Not a single instance is listed in which U.S. forces attempted to intervene directly in the affairs of other nations.

However, looking at the second one-hundred-plus-year period from 1898 to 2003, there were 202 instances of force, including the four types of operations listed previously and also seven others: (5) conventional operations, (6) peace operations, (7) noncombatant evacuation, (8) humanitarian relief, (9) resistance and counterinsurgency, (10) counter drug, and (11) counterterrorism. These figures do not include the normal stationing of forces worldwide, which has also grown substantially with the stationing of U.S. military forces in countries such as Korea and Germany during the Cold War, or the long-term "post conflict" operations in Iraq and Afghanistan as part of the Global War of Terror following the 9/11 attacks. As an exclamation point on this outward strategic focus, consider that in 2005, the U.S. Army had on a steady basis more than 250,000 soldiers deployed in more than 120 countries.[5] If the other military departments were included, the total would approach almost five hundred thousand American servicemen and women deployed on a daily basis.

This second one-hundred-year period provides ample evidence of the change in U.S. national security strategy in which the focus has become increasingly outward. Unlike in the first period, when there was not a single incident where U.S. forces attempted to intervene directly in the affairs of others, the second period has numerous instances reflecting U.S. intervention, such as the U.S. invasions of Korea (1950), Vietnam (1964), Panama (1989), Haiti (1994), and Bosnia (1995). This period is also significant as the United States transitioned from an isolationist nation, to a global power, to a superpower, and finally to the world's only hyperpower by the end of the twentieth century. With each transition, the United States became more involved in global affairs to include alliance leadership during the Cold War and finally global leadership in the post–Cold War period.

To illustrate the growing complexity of the national security environment and greatly increased comprehension required of the national security strategist, consider that in the early years of U.S. security strategy, the requirement was only for mastering the ground and maritime spheres of operation. In World War I, the air domain was added. During the Cold War, space as a medium of operations once again caused an expansion of the areas of concern. Now as the world enters the Information Age, the cyber domain has emerged as the latest area requiring the attention and comprehension of the strategist. This cyber world of influence would not be complete without adding the mastery of the temporal and informational aspects of this new era. Time and ideas are two non-physical areas of influence that have become at least as important, if not more so, to the development of strategy in the Information Age than their physical domain counterparts.

As a harbinger of the extraordinary expansion in the complexity of the national security field, consider the growth in the number of people that now have demonstrated or expressed concern for national security. The traditional list of the key players in the national security field include, for the executive branch, the principals and staff of the president, vice president, secretary of state, secretary of defense, secretary of energy, director of Central Intelligence, director of the Federal Bureau of Investigation, and the attorney general, to name a few. Congress and the Supreme Court also have significant roles resourcing the strategies and policies of the country and interpreting the Constitution, respectively. For both Congress and the Supreme Court, their national security component has increased with the emergence of the Information Age and the resultant globalization, and the events of 9/11. But what about the businessperson or the owner of the local mall? Are they part of the national security leadership apparatus of the country? I believe the answer is yes.

September 11 has caused a fundamental reevaluation of the roles and responsibilities of average Americans to the point where the tentacles of the national security system have reached down into the realm of non-traditional actors. The plant manager must now worry not only about meeting production quotas or keeping workers safe from accidents, but also about such things as evacuation plans in the event of mass casualties and providing portable respirators to workers for use in the event of an attack. Even the way in which the average American thinks about security has changed. In a sense, we are all cogs in the wheels of the national security apparatus. All of us now have become human intelligence collectors for the national security system. We are asked by our government to watch for actions that look out of place and given explicit directions on who to call and how to react if an anomaly is observed. While that does not necessarily make of all of us national security leaders, it certainly defines new roles and responsibilities for the individual in a free and open democratic society.

The costs of providing security and defense in the early years of the twenty-first century have also risen greatly. In 1996, the budget for the Department of Defense was below $300 billion per year. As of 2005, the United States spends over half a trillion dollars on defense. In terms of gross domestic product (GDP), defense spending has gone from just below 3 percent to just shy of 4 percent. Furthermore, if one believes that security and defense are not just about Department of Defense (DoD) contributions and thus must be considered more broadly, then the budgets of other participants, including the Department of Homeland

Security, Department of State, the Intelligence Community, the Department of Justice, and many others must also be considered. So in this broadened formulation, perhaps three quarters of a trillion dollars at the federal level alone goes into security and defense. These numbers do not begin to address the totals spent at the state and local levels. Certainly well over a trillion dollars is spent per year in the security and defense of the country.

Consider also the growth of *risk* in this highly globalized world. Putting together a successful attack given the proliferation of means, the increasing ability to interact globally, and the relative ease of coordinating in this new cyber environment have essentially changed the time-space relationships. One no longer needs to travel great distances to attack a target; it is possible to have a devastating impact on nations and economies with cyber attacks from thousands of miles away for the price of a low-end computer and Internet connection. And even in attacks where proximity is required, such as suicide bombings, increased capabilities of means translates to fewer "forward deployed" personnel executing even more deadly attacks. In Madrid in 2002, four bombs in satchels killed 191 people. This translates to increased risk to the intended targets of potential attacks. Even the resources necessary to execute the attacks of 9/11 were relatively modest compared with the amount spent on defense. Estimates from the 9/11 Commission report were that the attacks cost the perpetrators approximately $500,000, while the direct and indirect losses from the 9/11 attacks were estimated to cost well into the tens of billions of dollars and were felt well beyond New York State or U.S. national borders.

As the *environment*, *ends*, *ways*, *means*, and *risk* evolve over time, it follows that complementary changes in the leaders that execute strategy will also be required. But are these changes taking place? What should be done in the Information Age to mitigate the negative effects of globalization and better protect America and our allies?

The growing sophistication of the Information Age mandates that the twenty-first-century leader have a broader, and in some cases a different, set of tools available. This leader must be able to deal with the range of threats that will undoubtedly include the traditional challenges as well as the highly complex threats that are emerging. Response time will be highly compressed and a failure to act immediately in some cases will constitute the inaction that will expose seams and contribute to the success of the enemy. Decision cycles will be shortened, leaving less time to make the proper decision and execute a defensive solution to protect the nation's security. The Information Age leader must also learn to embrace complexity and ambiguity. The chaos that comes in this sort of uncertain world must be transformed from a disadvantage to overwhelming superiority. Inherent in this new leader is the development of environmental sensitivity. Some may equate this to cultural sensitivity, but I believe that it is much broader than purely being able to understand various cultures—it is the ability to sense and comprehend the total environment, to act under conditions of uncertainty, and to rapidly respond to the challenges and opportunities of the environment.

All in all, the national security leader will face more uncertainty and ambiguity than his or her predecessors and will be required to make assessments and act on those assessments more rapidly with far more at stake given the increasing capabilities of the means available to the potential adversary.

CHAPTER 2

Lists of Lists

Leadership is getting people to do things even when they really don't want to. . . .

—Unnamed congressman in meeting, May 2005

Influencing people by providing purpose, direction, and motivation—while operating to accomplish the mission and improving the organization.

—Army Field Manual 22-100, Leadership[1]

What the Experts Say

Defining leadership is a little like defining pornography: "I'll know it when I see it." Certainly anyone asked what leadership is could begin to rattle off a list of qualities or attributes of a leader. These lists would undoubtedly include values, human and technical skills, the ability to communicate and motivate, and the ability to organize and direct the efforts of others.

Asked to name people they considered leaders, most would have no difficulty producing a list of those individuals they considered to be leaders or have demonstrated leadership. Given the broad question, the list of leaders would include individuals from a wide variety of circles, from national and international leaders to people they had come in contact with throughout their lives, perhaps a relative or some other influential person. Many of the lists might even include a respected athlete. If the question were more narrowly focused on national security leaders, the list would likely be fairly predictable, including presidents and other well-known politicians from our history or from contemporary society; several may also identify community, religious, and military leaders. However, if asked to examine the characteristics and circumstances that made the people in their lists great leaders, I suspect that many would have great difficulty in identifying the nature of the leadership that propelled these individuals to the top of their lists.

For example, many Americans are likely to include in their list presidents such as George Washington, Thomas Jefferson, Abraham Lincoln, Ulysses S. Grant, Woodrow Wilson, Dwight Eisenhower, or John F. Kennedy. But if pressed to provide the rationale for their inclusion, few would be able to get past a line or two about the accomplishments of the person.

George Washington was the father of the country. Thomas Jefferson was a drafter of the Declaration of Independence and Constitution. Abraham Lincoln navigated the country through the difficult years of the Civil War when the nation's existence was very much in question. Ulysses S. Grant was a great Civil War general who later went on to become president of the United States. We could go on and on with this drill but get no closer to the essence of leadership and why these individuals might have been selected for inclusion in your list or why they were elected president.

The real question is, what is it about these men that made them great leaders? Are we to assume that since they were elected to the highest office in the land that they are worthy of inclusion? Is there or should there be some sort of criteria that elevates a person into the category of leader?

And what about others such as Susan B. Anthony and Martin Luther King, Jr., who championed for women's suffrage and civil rights, respectively? What made them leaders and propelled them to the forefront? Can we and should we consider them to be national security leaders? Certainly a good case can be made for their inclusion in this category by virtue of the effect they had on civil society in America and by extension on the security and defense of the nation. However, despite their inclusion in the national security leadership category, how many could truly articulate what made them leaders?

So we come full circle with the assertion that discussions of leadership invariably default to listing of the attributes and characteristics of a leader because leadership is so difficult to define. While many have tried to define leadership and to put a fine point on what makes a leader, identification of a leader is considerably easier than defining the mechanisms by which the leader leads.

Perhaps even more perplexing is that leadership is not an exact science. Even the experts do not necessarily agree about leaders and leadership. Theories abound, but unlike science, in which there are laws and properties, leadership seemingly cannot be reduced to a set of principles that, if followed, automatically make a person a leader.

In *Concepts of Leadership* by Don Clark, the author advances three theories of leadership including trait, great events, and transformational leadership theories.[2] In *Classical Leadership* by M. E. Doyle and M. K. Smith, the authors discuss four theories of leadership, including trait, behavioral, contingency, and transformational theories.[3] So which reference is right? Or is either of them right?

Actually, much common ground exists between the two lists such that there is an ability to cross-reference the two sets of theories. But the more important point is that leadership is not a science and does not have a finite body of knowledge that defines the study of leadership or the leader. Special relationships that exist between the leader and the organization clearly matter. Each organizational or leadership situation is likely to be very different. Techniques that work in one situation may lead to failure in another, and success in one field does not necessarily translate to success in another. Different fields may require a different type of leader, or at least an adaptability of the leader. This would explain why a leader in one field may be a follower in another.

Using the Smith and Doyle formulation of leadership theories, one can begin to apply definition and structure to this thing called leadership. In trait theory, the concept is that a well-defined list of attributes exists that presupposes leadership. Here the authors offer a list provided by John

Gardner, who conducted a study of North American organizations and leaders and concluded that a list of leadership traits could be developed (see table 1).[4] But is this the absolute list? Apparently not, since without too much trouble, one can find other lists of traits and qualities that could define a leader.

In *The Leadership Challenge* by James Kouzes and Barry Posner, another list of leader traits that will lead to successful leadership is presented.[5] The U.S. Army also provides several references that present lists of attributes, including *Military Leadership*[6] and *Leadership and Command at Senior Levels*.[7] The first reference provides an introduction to leadership and is more narrowly focused on entry-level leadership skills, while the second U.S. Army reference clearly examines the question of leadership for the senior ranks of the army. In his book *On Becoming a Leader,* Warren Bennis compares and contrasts leaders and managers, providing a useful listing of the qualities and attributes he values in leadership.[8]

Despite these enumerations of leadership traits, one likely feels no closer to understanding successful leadership. Even with the clarity of the five references, together they list almost sixty traits that assist in defining leaders and leadership. Granted, some overlap and thus the total number is probably less than thirty, but still, trying to apply thirty different leadership principles would probably still not allow one to arrive at the leadership "recipe." Even trying to distill the list to ten traits would be a challenge.

Perhaps the more relevant question would be whether this or any other distillation would produce the Holy Grail of leadership. I would suspect not, since leadership is not only about the leader any more than national security is only about defense. Other elements can and must play a role in the leadership equation. This is where the other leadership theories begin to surface.

The other obvious negative connotation with a pure trait theory formulation of leadership concerns the question of whether an individual must be born with the hardwiring for leadership or whether the important traits of leadership can be acquired through training, education, and experiences. This question will be examined in greater detail later; however, if one buys into the born leader theory, then the other 99 percent of society that become leaders through situational imperatives are destined to be second-class leaders. Overall, there is little evidence of the-pure born leader sub-theory.

Behavior theory, based on the notion that a leader balances concern for task with concern for people, and directive with participative leadership styles, establishes a formulation of leadership consisting of four quadrants in which leaders operate. The managerial grid established by Robert Blake and Janse Mouton in 1985 describes quite nicely the leadership styles in this manner.[9]

The individual with a low focus on task and personnel is labeled the improvised leader. One can only imagine the organization under the direction of this type of individual. Little direction is provided for the organization, and nothing even remotely resembling long-range organizational goals is provided. As a double shot against the organization, the leadership style results in a detached leader with little personal investment in the organization. Any achievements of the organization occur in spite of rather than because of this type of leader.

The individual with a low focus on task but a high focus on people receives the label of the "country club" leader. This type of leader places greater emphasis on rewards and relationships than on the accomplishment of organizational objectives. The name is quite fitting, since the climate set by the head of the organization reflects a more collegial leadership environment. The problems arise when the country club leader needs to pick up the pace to meet a deadline or to respond very quickly to new requirements. The leader may not be able to gain the response necessary if the organization cannot get out of the country club mode and into a more task-focused execution style.

The leader in the third quadrant has high focus on task and low focus on people. This leader pays little attention to the individuals or organization being led. The leader directs rather than leads the organization—this distinction is subtle, yet very important to understanding the cost in the long run of operating in this manner. The authoritarian, or autocratic, leader remains oblivious to what is going on beneath the surface so long as the mission is getting accomplished and the interpersonal relationships do not become dysfunctional and get in the way of output. Interestingly, a significant drawback to this type of leadership style, in addition to the

Table 1. Leadership Traits

Gardner	Kouzes & Posner	U.S. Army	Bennis
• Physical vitality and stamina • Intelligence and action oriented judgment • Eagerness to accept responsibility • Task competence • Understanding followers and their needs • Skill in dealing with people • Need for achievement • Capacity to motivate people • Courage and resolution • Trustworthiness • Decisiveness • Self-confidence • Assertiveness • Adaptability/ flexibility	• Challenge the process: find a process that you believe needs to be improved the most • Inspire a shared vision: share your vision in words that can be understood by your followers • Enable others to act: give them tools and methods to solve problems • Model the way: when the process gets tough, get your hands dirty • Encourage the heart: share the glory with your followers' heart, while keeping the pains within your own	*Principles of Leadership* • Know yourself and seek self-improvement • Be technically proficient • Seek responsibility and take responsibility for your actions • Make sound and timely judgments • Set the example • Know your people and look out for their well-being • Keep your workers informed • Develop a sense of responsibility in your workers • Ensure tasks are understood, supervised, and accomplished • Train as a team • Use the full capabilities of the team *Senior Levels* • Conceptual o Decision making o Forecasting o Creativity o Intuition • Competency o Perspective o Endurance o Risk taking o Coordination o Assessment • Communications o Interpersonal o Listening o Language o Teaching o Persuasion	• The manager administers; the leader innovates • The manager is a copy; the leader is an original • The manager maintains; the leader develops • The manager focuses on systems and structure; the leader focuses on people • The manager relies on control; the leader inspires trust • The manager has a short-range view; the leader has a long-range perspective • The manager asks how and when; the leader asks what and why • The manager has his or her eye always on the bottom line; the leaders' eye is on the horizon • The manager imitates; the leader originates • The manager accepts the status quo; the leader challenges it • The manager is the classic good soldier; the leader is his or her own person • The manager does things right; the leader does the right thing

detrimental effect on the morale and esprit of the organization, is that the organization tends to be adrift in the absence of the leader. Without direction from the top, the productivity diminishes.

The fourth type of leader in the behavioral theory is the team leader, who has a high focus on both the task and the people. Traits of this type of leader include the ability to balance the mission with the human needs of the individuals in the organization. Both the organization and its leaders are goal oriented, but also place a premium on the development of subordinates, sometimes even sub-optimizing on the outcome to train and educate subordinates, allowing them to gain valuable experience.

The discussion of the behavioral theory of leadership implies that the four quadrants are mutually exclusive and that leaders operate in one of the four quadrants only. In truth, most leaders tend to operate near the intersection of the four quadrants and move from left to right or up to down depending on the situation. There may be times when a leader operates more in the authoritarian role when time is of the essence despite his or her natural propensity to operate more as a team leader. In thinking of my own experiences in organizations both as a subordinate and a leader, I cannot think of too many leaders who were authoritarian all the time or full-time country club managers, at least not those that I considered to be successful leaders.

The contingency theory closely aligns with the behavior theory and the great events theory postulated by Don Clark. The crux of the contingency theory reflects the notion that situations arise that cause an individual to respond to accomplish goals and objectives of the organization. Effective leadership depends on a mix of factors, including the traits of the leader and the composition of the organization. Some may regard this as leadership by filling a vacuum. An example that comes to mind is the combat situation where the leader is killed or incapacitated on the battlefield and a soldier steps forward to take charge of the mission and ensure its success.

The last of the theories of leadership is transformation theory, which is based on the premise that anyone can become a leader and learn leadership styles. "The transformational leader: (1) raises our level of awareness, our level of consciousness about the significance and value of designated outcomes, and ways of reaching them, (2) gets us to transcend our own self-interest for the sake of the team, organization or larger polity, and (3) alters our need level (after Maslow) and expands our range of wants and needs."[10] While it should come as no surprise, the transformational theory of leadership has developed the widest following.

In truth, when one watches a leader in action, discerning whether one is watching a natural born leader, a behavioral leader, a situational or contingency leader, or a transformational leader is generally of little concern. What is most important is the relationship between the leader and the organization, whether the organization is successful and whether organizations and individuals are able to perform to their full potential. The definitive establishment of the leader's methodology is rarely of much import. Furthermore, most leaders would be hard pressed to spout theories of leadership, aside from the point made earlier that discussions of leadership inevitably result in a discussion of leader traits and perhaps anecdotal information about what made certain leaders and organizations a success.

And the Practitioners

In the previous section, several theories of leadership were advanced. Not to denigrate the work of the behavioral scientists or management experts, but a useful excursion is to see what the leadership practitioner, the leader, has to say about leadership. For every leader, one is likely to find a distinct formulation of leadership. With this in mind, my purpose is to review a cross section of national security leaders from across the ages with a particular focus on American leaders, although we will begin our examination with two non-American practitioners.

Sun Tzu was a Chinese philosopher, general, and author. He lived almost 2,500 years ago, although the exact date remains unknown. He lived and fought for the kingdom of Wu in the feudal society of China and wrote a text that documented the lessons of the kingdom over a period of some two decades during which the armies of Wu were undefeated in battle. His work, *The Art of War*, remains important today because it represents the earliest known writings on the subject of strategy. He wrote of the political and military, of warfare and the state, and of leaders and organizations.

Sun Tzu theorized that "the art of war was governed by five constant factors, all of which need to be taken into account. They are: the Moral Law; Heaven; Earth; the Commander; Method; and Discipline."[11]

Both the moral law and the commander pertain directly to the art of leadership in Sun Tzu's strategy. He states, "The Moral Law causes the people to be in complete accord with their ruler, so that they will follow him regardless of their lives, undismayed by any danger,"[12] and "The Commander stands for the virtues of wisdom, sincerity, benevolence, courage and strictness."[13] The two statements together provide insights into the relationship between the army and its general. The army owes loyalty and discipline, while the leader owes the personal qualities and capabilities necessary to do battle over extended distances for long periods of time while protecting the forces and accomplishing the required missions.

The Art of War contains numerous recommendations, observations, and imperatives concerning the strategic and tactical employment of forces against an enemy. Consider, for example:

> *On warfare*: To fight and conquer in all your battles is not supreme excellence; supreme excellence consists of breaking the enemy's resistance without fighting.[14]
>
> *On defeating the enemy*: The skillful leader subdues the enemy's troops without any fighting; he captures their cities without laying siege to them; he overthrows their kingdom without lengthy operations in the field. With his forces intact he disputes the mastery of empire, and thus, without losing a man, his triumph is complete.[15]
>
> *On generalship*: The general is the bulwark of the state: if the bulwark is strong at all points, the state will be strong; if the bulwark is defective, the state will be weak.[16]
>
> *On span of control*: The control of a large force is the same in principle as the control of a few men; it is merely a question of dividing up the numbers.[17]
>
> *On deception*: All warfare is based on deception. Hence, when we are able to attack we must seem unable; when using our forces, we must seem unable; when we are near, we must make the enemy believe we are far away.[18]

> *On knowing the situation*: If you know the enemy and know yourself, you need not fear the result of a hundred battles. If you know yourself but not the enemy, for every victory gained you will suffer a defeat. If you know neither the enemy nor yourself, you will succumb in every battle.[19]

The passages above highlight the link between strategy and the leader. In Sun Tzu's depiction of strategy, everything flows from the leader. The ability to amass forces at the necessary time, the ability to understand the situation and to determine whether to attack or feint, and, most importantly, the strength of a state and its people are all directly related to the strength of its leader. The intellectual work that accompanies the physical act of battle also resides in the realm of the leader. Those that understand human nature and can translate this knowledge into action (or inaction, as in the case of defeating the enemy without offering battle) will prevail.

Carl von Clausewitz, a German military strategist who wrote of the campaigns of the Napoleonic era in a book titled *On War*, also describes the relationship between the strategy and the leader and between the military art and the general. The volume, published posthumously by his wife, is a compendium of eight books dealing with topics on strategy and warfare including the nature and theory of war, strategy, engagement, military forces, the defense, the attack, and war plans. In book 1, Clausewitz prominently features a chapter titled "On Military Genius" that investigates the role of the leader in strategic and military operations.

It should come as no surprise that direct and concentrated discussions of leadership would come in the beginning of this volume; for Clausewitz, the commander occupies a central position in the outcome of grand strategy and military operations. He unabashedly presents the concept of "gifts of the mind and temperament," which constitute the essence of military genius.[20]

In this critical chapter, Clausewitz addresses several key ingredients for the leader, including intellectual powers and courage in making decisions. He states,

> Two qualities are indispensable: first an intellect that, even in the darkest hour, retains the glimmerings of inner light which leads to

> truth; and second, the courage to follow this faint light wherever it may lead. The first of these qualities is described as *coup d'oeil*; the second is determination.[21]

This notion of *coup d'oeil* is fascinating as it refers to having an innate ability to see and understand. Today we are more likely to talk about terms such as "being able to visualize the strategy" or "the battlespace." Within this passage, Clausewitz devotes considerable attention to the intellectual prowess expected of a commander. He opines that the leader must not only be able to see and understand the situation, but also to discern what changes to the original plans are required and how best to implement them. Of course, in the Clausewitzian formulation, the span of control and the manner of executing changes is far less complicated given the reality of Napoleonic warfare, which frequently encompassed thousands of soldiers lined up shoulder to shoulder in large phalanx formations. In contrast, today the density of soldiers in a kilometer frontage can at times be counted on the fingers of a single hand. An equally important conclusion affirms that "to bring a war, or one of its campaigns, to a successful close requires a thorough grasp of national policy. On the level of strategy and policy coalescence: the commander-in-chief is the statesman."[22]

Clausewitz also identifies the personal characteristics "energy, firmness, staunchness, emotional balance, and strength of character" as central to the leader. Without these fundamentals, he asserts that the leader will not effectively control and direct the efforts of the strategy.

No discussion of great leaders would be complete without at least some mention of George Washington, who is widely recognized as the father of our country. Washington was highly successful in all aspects of his life. Despite lack of a formal education, Washington was an explorer, surveyor, farmer, businessman, general, politician, and finally, the first president of the United States. First offered the title "king," he had the wisdom, forethought, and even the humility to see that the country needed an elected president, not an appointed monarch.

Philip E. Schoenberg, an expert on the American presidents, discusses twelve leadership lessons George Washington exhibited during his time as an early American leader.[23]

Washington's Leadership Lessons

1. Set high goals by having a vision.
2. Set an example by becoming a role model.
3. Choose a mentor.
4. Be a lifelong learner.
5. Doing the little things leads to the big things.
6. Be a great communicator.
7. Learn from failures and mistakes.
8. Have the courage of your convictions by believing in yourself.
9. Know how to make a decision.
10. Be a team leader.
11. Show compassion.
12. Quit while you're ahead.

The character and determination of Washington's leadership is worthy of study and emulation. Consider the enormity of the task before the Founding Fathers and George Washington in particular. A group of unorganized, ill-equipped, and in some regards unguided gentlemen with little or no experience in governance banded together to plant the seeds of freedom and democracy in America. Their mission was to break with the British Crown and form a new nation based on the concept of equality and liberty and justice for all.

Despite several defeats in battle, Washington persevered and learned from failure. It is this determination and strength of character that remained a constant in his life and allowed him to achieve great wealth, fame, and lasting recognition of his special place in American history. Perhaps no American general was ever challenged more than George Washington was as he molded a raggedy band of protesters into an army on the fields of Cambridge Common in Massachusetts.

Washington was also quite the innovator. In his personal and professional life, he continuously sought growth. Schoenberg writes,

> As an innovative farmer, he introduced alfalfa and mules to America. As a businessman, he invested in factories and canals. As a general, he could make life and death decisions quickly in the heat of battle.

> As president, he had the luxury of time in the slow transportation and communications of the day to take his time to make up his mind. As president, he consulted his cabinet on a regular basis.[24]

He was able to see above the everyday to look into the future to see great opportunities, and was not afraid to embrace, even direct, change.

Lincoln on Leadership, by Donald T. Phillips, provides fascinating insights into the leadership of our thirteenth president.[25] Abraham Lincoln was reputed to be a man of modest means, great humility, patience, absolute integrity, innovation, and extraordinary wit. He was also considered to be "a second rate lawyer with no leadership experience" at the time of his election in 1860.[26]

In many respects, Lincoln was the ideal leader to negotiate the difficulties of our Civil War and to bring a divided nation back together when victory was assured. His influence can be seen on the prosecution of the war and the post-conflict settlements; he remained fully engaged in the conflict, but detached enough to allow the field commanders—once the right commanders were identified—the latitude to execute their plan. Certainly his difficulties with the string of Union Army commanders were well known, but his ability to make the necessary changes to establish the right chain of command demonstrates great courage. His absolute focus on the outcome was another important component of his leadership strategy. Despite setbacks early in the Civil War, Lincoln never wavered from his vision of a united nation.

The table of contents from Phillips's book provides an important overview of Lincoln's philosophy. If one were relating Lincoln's theory of leadership to the theories discussed previously, elements of the trait, behavior, contingency, and transformational theories can be easily discerned (see table 2).

Personal characteristics held an important place in Lincoln's leadership style; he seemingly never forgot the traits that propelled him to the presidency. In his dealings with key Union generals, he was able to be both nurturing as well terse and direct. Because he led the country through the national emergency of the Civil War, Lincoln rose to greatness perhaps even higher than he would have envisioned. He also demonstrated the ability to embrace change and instill innovation, whether through the changing of commanders or in the battle plans that he approved.

At the end of the day, Lincoln's leadership came down to three key traits. He knew how to inspire people to do their best. He admitted and learned from his mistakes, and adapted and innovated as necessary. Finally, Lincoln had an inner vision of himself that his detractors could not be shake.

Table 2. Lincoln's Leadership

People	▪ Get out of the office and circulate among the troops ▪ Build strong alliances ▪ Persuade rather than coerce
Character	▪ Honesty and integrity are the best policies ▪ Never act out of vengeance or spite ▪ Have the courage to handle unjust criticism
Endeavor	▪ Exercise a strong hand—be decisive ▪ Lead by being led ▪ Set goals and be results oriented ▪ Keep searching until you find your "Grant" ▪ Encourage innovation
Communication	▪ Master the art of public speaking ▪ Influence people through conversation and storytelling ▪ Preach a vision and continually reaffirm it

The leadership traits of two Civil War generals—Robert E. Lee and Ulysses S. Grant, the leaders of the Confederate and Union forces respectively, by the Civil War's end—provide an interesting comparison and contrast in leadership styles.

Robert E. Lee was the son of a Henry "Light-Horse Harry" Lee, a cavalry officer who had fought in the Revolutionary War. He graduated from the United States Military Academy in 1829 with both academic and leadership honors, graduating second and achieving the highest leadership position in his class. Early in his career he saw action in combat during the Mexican-American War, where he served under the legendary Gen. Winfield Scott. Lee's actions in the battles of Cerro Gordo, Churubusco, and Chapultepec earned him accelerated promotions and a well-deserved reputation for leadership and courage under fire.

He has been credited with an innate ability to understand the broader context of each of the battles in which he fought. This *coup d'oeil* would serve him well later in his military career as the leader of the Confederate Army. Another important leadership characteristic that became evident was Lee's skill at "working with others and within the system to get what he wanted."[27]

Despite being offered command of the Union Army by President Lincoln, Lee chose to remain loyal to his native Virginia and accepted a commission in and eventually command of the Confederate Army. As commander of the Army of Northern Virginia, Lee had several early successes in battle, including the battles of Seven Days, second Bull Run, Fredericksburg, and Chancellorsville. Unfortunately, the cost of these victories in total numbers and in capable commanders proved too much to sustain.

He was considered to be a master tactician and strategist, yet the overextension of his lines certainly contributed to the ultimate demise of the Army of Northern Virginia. In particular, the decision to seek battle at Gettysburg demonstrates the results of this indiscretion.

On a personal level, he was a man to be revered. Lee was deeply religious, considered himself to be a family man, although he spent far less time with his family than he desired, and had a persona that inspired confidence. As a result, in many regards Lee has achieved a larger-than-life status. Men and women were known to line the streets to get a glimpse of Lee riding into town. His men cheered him and fought more bravely in his presence. Even in the face of defeat, his subordinates refused to blame him.

By contrast, Grant was an average soldier in his early years. His great battles with alcoholism seem just as legendary as some of the important Civil War battles. Also a graduate of the United States Military Academy, his early years lacked distinction, and he certainly failed to show the promise of Lee.

Grant fought in the Mexican-American War as well, but failed to garner much notice or attract much positive professional attention. In fact, it is during this period that Grant's difficulties with alcohol first surfaced, and his alcoholism only became worse after the Mexican-American War with his reassignment to San Francisco as a quartermaster officer. Schoenberg writes,

> Grant had resigned from the U.S. Army because of a drinking problem; then he failed as a farmer in Missouri and in managing his father's leather goods store in Galena, Illinois. When the Civil War broke out, Grant returned to service his country and got a second chance to resume his military career.[28]

It is in this second chance that Grant got another opportunity and Lincoln found his commander. Virtually every account of Grant discusses his sense of purpose and aggressive nature while serving as commander of the Union Army. While little from his first military career demonstrated his sense of vision, his development of a coherent battle plan that saw the war as "single battlefield and no longer based the Union strategy solely on the capture of Richmond" must be recognized as a brilliant strategic maneuver.[29] His aggressive nature also became evident in his battle plan, which focused on destroying the Confederate armies in detail to weaken the enemy's capabilities and finally break its resolve.

During the Civil War and immediately thereafter, Grant demonstrated some of his greatest leadership qualities. While mastery of the physical elements of battle, the preparation of forces, provisioning of an army, and the planning for battle were certainly key to the Union victory, his personal abilities as a leader must be recognized as well.

Grant was an inspiration to his men, although not on the same level as Lee. He was also known as a commander that chose great subordinates and provided adequate direction without overmanaging their efforts or battle plans. Schoenberg's assessment of Grant's leadership style is critical to understanding the central role he played in the ultimate defeat of the Confederate forces:

> Grant empowered his subordinates. He believed that the best managers were those who could think for themselves. Grant helped his subordinates realize a shared sense of purpose through discussion of the objectives and how each of those objectives were to be implemented. Even in his detailed orders, he wrote they should take advantage of enemy's weaknesses and retreats without waiting for orders.[30]

On a personal level, Grant demonstrated not only great tenacity on the battlefield, but also great compassion. Numerous accounts speak to the kind and gentle manner in which Grant treated soldiers from the vanquished Confederate armies and his nemesis, General Lee. The simple, yet important, gestures of allowing the officers to retain possession of their personal belongings and for the Confederate soldiers to be paroled rather than held as prisoners provide ample evidence of compassionate nature.

His Civil War experiences did little to prepare him for the role of president of the United States. Although he served two terms as president, accounts of this time yield mixed reviews. As a president, Grant never truly grew into the role. His administration was tainted by scandals and malaise. The White House's official website makes the following unflattering observations:

> He was, as the symbol of Union victory during the Civil War, their logical candidate for President in 1868. When he was elected, the American people hoped for an end to turmoil. Grant provided neither vigor nor reform. Looking to Congress for direction, he seemed bewildered. One visitor to the White House noted "a puzzled pathos, as of a man with a problem before him of which he does not understand the terms."[31]

Lee and Grant certainly provide an interesting contrast in leadership. While considering the leadership theories discussed previously, Lee looks to fit more into the trait theory and thus to have achieved much of his success through force of personality, while Grant was more closely aligned with the great events or situational leadership theory. Despite his election to the highest office of the land, Grant never again achieved the greatness that he displayed as commander of the Union Army.

The World War II era produced some of the most recognizable and colorful national security leaders in our nation's history. The great events or situational theory of leadership applied to key leaders such as U.S. Army Generals Douglas MacArthur, George C. Marshall, and Dwight Eisenhower; U.S. Navy Admirals Chester W. Nimitz and William Halsey; and U.S. Air Force General Curtis LeMay.

If anyone can be said to personify the trait theory, it was Douglas MacArthur. Son of an army general, he went to the United States Military Academy at West Point where he enjoyed considerable success, graduating first in his class and serving as the first captain of the Corps of Cadets during his final year. His army career was filled with top assignments, including aide to the president of the United States. Quite early in his career, he served in World War I and distinguished himself on the battlefield, receiving numerous awards for gallantry and wounds suffered in battle.

Perhaps the latter part of his army career most distinguished MacArthur as a great leader as he went on to lead the dogged island-hopping campaign in the Pacific theater. His pledge to return to the Philippines even as he was being evacuated from the island nation under considerable enemy pressure and his eventual return remain vivid symbols of the determination of the American cause. Following World War II, MacArthur oversaw the reconstruction of Japan, including the political, economic, military, and social reforms of the conquered nation. His final significant contribution to U.S. defense came as United Nations (UN) commander of allied forces in Korea during the Korean War. MacArthur was eventually relieved of command by President Truman for criticizing U.S. policies in the war.

A discussion of World War II leaders would not be complete without mention of Gen. George C. Marshall, perhaps the quintessential soldier-statesman. A graduate of Virginia Military Institute, Marshall was very senior at the beginning of the war and was serving as the chief of staff of the army. In this role, the responsibility for manning, training, and equipping the army was his. The fact that he did not serve overseas in the war resulted from his indispensability to President Franklin Roosevelt as a senior military adviser. He is largely credited as one of the key architects of the war, and thus received great accolades for the American success in campaign planning and execution.

Following retirement, he went on to a successful career of public service, which included positions as the secretary of state and head of the Red Cross. The Marshall Plan, which he authored, became the cornerstone of initiatives to rebuild Europe following the devastation of the war and set the conditions for normalizing relations with vanquished foes. As an exclamation point to his service, Marshall was awarded the Nobel Peace Prize in 1953.

If MacArthur personified the trait theory, General Eisenhower was more closely aligned with the great events theory of leadership. Coming from a small town in Texas, there was little in his background that suggested that he would one day lead the largest allied invasion force of World War II and go on to become the president of the United States and leader of the free world.

General Eisenhower attended West Point but was an undistinguished scholar, athlete, and soldier there, graduating in the middle of his class. His army career was also somewhat undistinguished, although he developed a stream of mentors and acquaintances that would prove pivotal to preparing him for the essential role he would play as the Supreme Allied Commander during World War II in the European theater of operations.

First among equals in this regard was Gen. Fox Connor, who would coach Eisenhower in the art and science of the military. Eisenhower also served with or for Generals Pershing, MacArthur, and Patton. A further defining position was his year of study at the Command and General Staff College at Fort Leavenworth, where he graduated first in his class. These associations and the mentorship Eisenhower received, combined with his personality and his ability to forge a team, have largely been seen as the major contributing factors to the building and sustainment of the allied coalition in the European theater.

It is worthy of note that prior to the beginning of the war in 1939, Eisenhower was a lieutenant colonel who had never seen combat, yet some six years later by the end of the war he had risen to five-star rank and command of Allied Forces Europe. Following World War II, Eisenhower remained in Europe, overseeing the reconstruction efforts and waging the early stages of the Cold War. Upon his retirement, he was elected as the thirty-fourth president of the United States.

Of his special talents for team building that suited him so well in directing the European theater, Schoenberg writes,

> Time and again, Eisenhower demonstrated how he could inspire people to work together. He believed in team work from his early

> days as an assistant football coach when he was a cadet at West Point. As the head of allied armies in Europe, he managed to get British and American generals, all with great egos, to become a team during World War Two. He managed to get British Lord Montgomery and the American George Patton to work together. Charles De Gaulle, the French personification of ego, trusted Ike. After World War Two, Eisenhower then became the first head of NATO [North Atlantic Treaty Organization] where he got nine nations to cooperate in their common defense.[32]

Eisenhower's personal account of his life including his rise to prominence and his assessment of what shaped his success are well documented in an autobiography entitled, *At Ease: Stories I Tell Friends.* It should come as no surprise that the book, like the man himself, is humble and unassuming, despite his great achievements.

Admirals Nimitz and Halsey were graduates of the United States Naval Academy and became naval heroes of World War II in the Pacific. When examining their careers and the great success they achieved, one can clearly see the transformational leadership theory as dominating their rise. Both men were credited with developing new strategies and tactics of naval warfare that contributed immeasurably to the outcome in the Pacific. Nimitz was commander during two key naval engagements of the war, the Battles of Coral Sea and Midway. Of particular note are his contributions to the development of the island-hopping campaign in the Pacific and to fleet tactics that saw the incorporation of the aircraft carriers into offensive operations. Halsey was the commander of naval forces in the Pacific and oversaw the campaign in the Solomon Islands and the preparatory phases of the battle for the Philippines. He also commanded U.S. forces in Guadalcanal during this important offensive.

Gen. Curtis LeMay was another distinguished leader in World War II and its aftermath who clearly demonstrates transformational leadership qualities. At the beginning of the war, LeMay was bomber pilot in the U.S. Army Air Corps commanding the 305th Bombardment Group. By the war's end, he had developed new tactics for precision daylight and low level bombing. He had also designed a concept of strategic bombing that he would continue to refine throughout his career. LeMay was also credited with deploying the atomic bombs that were dropped over Hiroshima and Nagasaki and commanding the Berlin Airlift relief of Europe.

At the war's end and with the signing of the National Security Act of 1947, General LeMay oversaw the establishment of the air force as a separate service of the armed forces.[33] His contributions following the war as the commander of Strategic Air Command (SAC) and later as the chief of staff of the air force largely shaped the strategies and policies of his service over the course of Cold War.

The World War II period provides ample evidence of the diversity of senior leaders. No single element or set of traits emerges as dominant among these men, yet each made immeasurable contributions to the security and defense of the United States during a pivotal point in our nation's history.

The Reagan years also provide interesting insights into key national security leaders. President Ronald Reagan emerges as both an important and fascinating character. Despite little formal political training or education, Reagan was elected governor of California and later to the presidency for two terms. He is largely seen as having directed and overseen the rebuilding of the military after the malaise of Vietnam.

Several key initiatives during his presidency included the significant growth of the defense budget, which increased from $134 billion in 1980 to $290 billion in 1988; fielding of improved capabilities in all four services of the armed forces; recommitment of U.S. capabilities to NATO; fielding of offensive Pershing II ballistic missiles in Europe to counter the Soviet threat and establish a viable link to the U.S. nuclear strategic arsenal; and the end of the Cold War with the falling of the Berlin Wall and demise of the Warsaw Pact and the Soviet Union.

The Reagan years are also seen as key to meeting and defeating the communist or Marxist threat and promoting democracy. Important areas of confrontation during his presidency include Central America, Grenada, Angola, and Afghanistan. In his 1985 State of the Union Address, President Reagan stated, "We must stand by all our democratic allies," a pledge he certainly kept throughout his presidency. Quotes that personify Reagan's leadership style include:

"The challenge of statesmanship is to have the vision to dream of a better, safer world and the courage, persistence, and patience to turn that dream into reality."
—March 8, 1985

". . . there is no limit to what a man can do or where he can go if he doesn't mind who gets the credit."
—January 21, 1981

"We in government should learn to look at our country with the eyes of the entrepreneur, seeing possibilities where others see only problems."
—January 26, 1985

"A leader, once convinced a particular course of action is the right one, must have the determination to stick with it and be undaunted when the going gets rough."
—December 5, 1990[34]

These statements give insight into the visionary qualities, determination, persistence, and character of the last president of the Cold War period. Reagan's extraordinary abilities to develop a vision, communicate it to the country and even the world, persist even in the face of overwhelming odds, and remain optimistic throughout that set him apart.

If Reagan was the visionary behind the return of American military might and defeat of communism, then Caspar Weinberger, his secretary of defense, was the key architect. Weinberger had served in two previous administrations under Presidents Nixon and Ford. As the secretary of defense, he was charged with running the Pentagon and overseeing the defense buildup of the 1980s. He also deserves credit for causing America to look hard at the issue of the commitment of forces.

In 1986, largely in response to the Vietnam experience, Secretary Weinberger and his staff developed a six-point checklist to identify the conditions under which the use of force was appropriate. The checklist was presented to Congress in the secretary's February 5, 1986, message. It included the following provisions: (1) U.S. forces should only be committed to combat in defense of interests vital to the nation or its allies, (2) U.S. forces should only be committed in numbers adequate to complete the mission, (3) U.S. forces should only be committed when there are clearly defined political and military objectives, (4) the relationship between objectives and forces committed should be continually reassessed and adjusted if necessary, (5) U.S. forces should be committed only when there is a reasonable assurance of support from the American people and Congress, and (6) U.S. forces should only be committed as a last resort.

The Weinberger Criteria, as these points became known, formed the basis for most of the deliberations concerning the use of force during the post–Cold War period, and have had resurgence following operations in Iraq in 2003.

While Colin Powell came to prominence at the end of the Reagan administration, the roots of his success can be traced to the early days of Reagan's presidency. Rising from modest means to four-star general, national security adviser, and finally secretary of state can be directly related to the mentorship, experiences, and education he received beginning with his participation as a White House fellow, where he first met Weinberger and Frank Carlucci.[35] He saw combat action in Vietnam and oversaw the U.S. military's intervention in Panama in 1989 and the first Gulf War in 1991.

Though they do not provide a definitive study of leadership, Powell's autobiography, *My American Journey*, lists a set of thirteen rules.[36] While they are simply labeled "Colin Powell's Rules," they read more like a set of leadership principles. As with the other practitioners that have been cited, common elements exist. Powell's list and the informed manner in which they are presented also provide insights into the man and his leadership style.

Colin Powell's Rules

1. It ain't as bad as you think. It will look better in the morning.
2. Get mad, then get over it.
3. Avoid having your ego so close to your position that when your position falls, your ego goes with it.
4. It can be done!
5. Be careful what you choose. You may get it.
6. Don't let adverse facts stand in the way of a good decision.
7. You can't make someone else's choices. You shouldn't let someone else make yours.
8. Check small things.

9. Share credit.
10. Remain calm. Be kind.
11. Have a vision. Be demanding.
12. Don't take counsel of your fears or naysayers.
13. Perpetual optimism is a force multiplier.

What lessons can these theorists and leaders teach us about leadership and strategy in the Information Age? Do the lessons of history remain relevant today?

The reader should be somewhat comforted by the fact that there is some general agreement between the theorists and the practitioners with regard to what is important in leadership. Common themes that emerge suggest that having a sense of purpose or vision and the ability to communicate it are important qualities. Also of great import in this business of leadership is the ability to motivate and inspire subordinates, organizations, and even a nation to reach for a shared purpose. Other important qualities are persistence, often in the face of great odds; optimism and spirit to provide momentum; and the ability to adapt and innovate to respond in the event that the leader's plan is not initially leading to the desired outcome.

It would be an understatement to lament that there is no single definitive source for all leaders in all situations.

An Equation for Leadership

The point of the previous discussion in this section is to highlight that in debates and considerations of leadership, the conversation often turns to a listing of the attributes that describe a leader in an effort to establish a template or define what qualities identify a person as a leader. While this is certainly not a completely wrong approach, it fails to fully capture the essence of leadership.

While not intending to fall into the trap of turning leadership into a pure science or meticulously defining leadership in terms of a mathematical equation, the elaboration of components of leadership can be useful as a baseline from which to later describe where the Information Age environment and the infusion of information technologies are likely to require complementary changes in leadership for this new national security environment. Thus to best illustrate what is different about leadership in the Information Age, as a baseline for the discussion, an equation describing the components of leadership will be adopted.

In *Executive Leadership,* by Elliott Jaques and Stephen D. Clement, the authors have developed an equation for determining what they term "current actual capability" (CAC), which is further defined as "leadership competence" (LC).[37] This CAC reflects the individual's ability to lead in a given situation at the time of the evaluation.

The equation developed by Jaques and Clement is

CAC = CP + V + K/S + Wi – T, where:

CP = Cognitive power (cognitive complexity, or the innate mental ability to organize information)

V = Values (interests, priorities)

K/S = Skilled use of relevant knowledge

Wi = Wisdom about people and things

T = Serious personality (temperamental) defects

The discussion advanced by Jaques and Clement is compelling because it allows for the idea that a leader can employ certain personal traits in varying levels to establish competent leadership, or, in the words of an army field manual, "influence people by providing purpose, direction, and motivation—while operating to accomplish the mission and improving the organization."[38] Furthermore, it seems reasonable that having basic skills such as cognitive power will at a minimum identify key requirements for leaders. Perhaps even more important is the recognition that an effective leader must not have temperament or personality defects that interfere with the execution of his or her leadership role.

Unlike the previous discussion in which lists of character traits were identified, the Jaques and Clement formula deals with broad categories such as cognitive capacity, personality, and values without specifying which exact characteristics are essential in the equation.

Before proceeding, some observations about the equation are in order. First, the current actual capability of any individual is not static and most certainly moves up or down depending on the new skills acquired through training, education, or experience. An individual's resultant capacity also varies depending on the type of leadership position in which the individual is involved. For example, an individual is highly likely to have vastly different CAC scores for leading as a college football coach versus serving as the CEO of a corporate law firm. Certainly both positions require leadership to be successful, but the mix of the various components of the equation will be very different for each.

For this reason, defining leadership in exact terms or in absolutes would be counterproductive. The leader and the requirements for leadership must vary based on the environment, the organization, and the mission to be accomplished. As well, the amount of each of the individual ingredients matters less than the capabilities of the whole person, examined in a cumulative manner. So if a person had some minor shortfalls in cognitive power, but was able to compensate in wisdom, then the cumulative capability could be approximately equivalent. This discussion is not meant to transform leadership into some type of recipe where the leader mixes one part X, one part Y, and two parts Z to arrive at the perfect leadership outcome. Rather, using this methodology may assist in identifying and understanding the important components of leadership.

Notice also the use of the word "minor" in the preceding paragraph. We must be realistic in our discussions of leadership. Certain entry-level capabilities will undoubtedly be required in certain fields. A 5'6" man with no basketball ability will not have much chance of being captain of a professional basketball team, any more than a non-college graduate would have to lead a prestigious law firm.

The other important aspect of looking at the Jaques and Clement equation is its use as a starting point to identify how leadership, particularly national security leadership, will need to change in the Information Age.

CHAPTER 3

Globalization and the Information Age

Describing the New National Security Environment

A ride at Disney World in Florida serves as a useful analogy for the Information Age. In this particular ride, the background and the passengers are traveling in opposite directions creating the illusion of speed. In preparation for the ride, passengers queue into a long, snaking line that plods along at a snail's pace. When the rider arrives at the front of the line, the floor is slowly moving, and the rider must climb into the car and get strapped into the moving vehicle while receiving last-minute instructions from the attendant. Almost immediately after this preparation is completed, the speed picks up and the car moves along the track at a constant and fairly controlled speed. Along the walls are scenes of the outdoors, creating the sensation of driving along a country road on a beautiful summer day. As the ride progresses, the background appears to move faster and faster. By the end of the five-minute ride, the participant has gone from near zero to the speed of space flight. It is an incredible sensation for the rider to be traveling around an enclosed track at a constant speed and have this illusion of great speed. All of the senses are piqued, and toward the end of the ride, the rider's ability to comprehend the surroundings is significantly degraded. To add to the confusion, if the rider closes his or her eyes, the world returns to the slow moving speed of the car in which they are riding.

However, by simply opening one's eyes, the illusion of speed returns. By the end of the ride in the simulation of space travel, there is simply too much information coming at the rider too quickly to realistically be absorbed. This same sensation provides an analogy for the Information Age leader. With so much information to be absorbed, how does the leader determine what is important in this highly confusing, data-dense, globalized Information Age world?

In *Securing America's Future: National Strategy in the Information Age,* twelve principles for national security in the Information Age are developed that describe the changes that globalization fueled by information technologies will cause. The principles and a brief overview of each are provided by way of an introduction to this new era. They are provided as a means to force the reader to consider the fundamental differences to be encountered by the twenty-first-century national security leader.

1. Globalization is a real force. Some have questioned whether the globalization exists or the degree to which it impacts the world in which we live. It should come as no surprise to the reader given the previous discussions of globalization that I believe it is the driving force behind changes in the human interactions that we are witnessing today. Information technologies are providing limitless access to vast amounts of information at a modest cost. The potential for increasing human productivity and improving quality of life are nearly infinite. In August 2005, reports were that the genome for rice, a staple crop for half the world, had been decoded. With this advancement, it would be possible to increase crop yields and feed more of the world's population. Internet cafés are appearing throughout the world, even in countries with authoritarian regimes. Imagine the impact in closed societies of having alternate sources of data besides the government from which to draw one's daily news and information. But globalization is also fueling instability and changing the essence of state-to-state relationships, creating transnational alliances such as the al Qaeda terror network. A true Information Age phenomenon worthy of consideration concerns the cost of information. Unlike any other commodity, the cost to acquire data and process it into usable information far outweighs the cost of distributing and copying the information. This fact will have significant impact on issues such as research and development, the protection of intellectual property rights, or even the spread of Information Age technologies.

2. The world is getting smaller. Not in a physical sense, but rather in a time, space, and ideological sense, the relationships we have come to know and understand are changing. The ability to traverse great distances by moving from point X to Y has increased, but conceptually, the need to traverse these distances has been mitigated through the use of information technologies. Why travel three hours by airplane to attend a conference when a video teleconference link can just as easily allow for this interaction? I have heard people ask questions about why events in another state or across the country or even halfway around the world matter. Previously, one could make the case that these events were not relevant and that we were isolated. However, with advances in transportation and communications, this case can no longer be made; it really does matter what happens, even in distant locations, as the spillover wrought by globalization can and will affect us.

3. The nature, character, and conduct of conflict are changing, as is the manner in which we think about it. Nations and even nonstate actors have a greater ability to engage in conflict. It is not even clear that the traditional manner of thinking about conflict as state-on-state or internally within states will hold in future conflicts—what about the case of transnational conflict where actors cross national boundaries, forming international coalitions of nonstate actors? Information technologies now allow for conflict to be waged at great distances, in contrast to the traditional manner of settling disputes where opposing forces met on the field of battle, as in Napoleonic warfare or during World War II. Consider also that whole new fields of conflict with farther-reaching and more dangerous potential, such as weapons of mass destruction capabilities and information operations, have emerged and proliferated.

4. The world is becoming more complex. The body of knowledge has grown exponentially. New fields such as nanotechnology, which combines information technology and biology, are emerging. New elements are being discovered and entered into the periodic table of elements, and some of these fundamental elements are synthetic. Even in the social sciences, such as international relations, increasing complexity is a fact that must be considered, as in the case of operations in Iraq that began in 2003. Given a greater number of actors adding more voices and thus more opinions, ground truth is nearly impossible to determine. The world not only watches coalition operations and insurgent attacks, but also has access to Web logs (blogs) that describe the combat action and report in real time on the reconstruction efforts. Each and every turn in the ongoing conflict is available and the access to raw data is unprecedented. It is not an overstatement to assert that the world is watching the building of a nation, the emergence of democracy, and of course any miscue like the inadvertent bombing of civilians as these events happen. Actors including the United States and the Coalition, the Iraqi people, nongovernmental organizations, the United Nations, regional and global powers, the media, and terrorist organizations all have opinions and interests that are expressed daily with regard to Iraq. But what is really happening? Sometimes it is difficult to tell from all of the information that is available.

5. There is a greater availability of means. The proliferation of means has made conflict available to states, nonstate organizations, and individuals. Weapons from small arms and explosives to major weapons systems such as submarines are available on the open market to the highest bidder. Even new ways to use systems intended for peaceful purposes can be "converted" for destructive or military purposes. Consider the use of four civilian aircraft as weapons of mass destruction on 9/11. One cannot just think of this proliferation in the sense of weapons and in the physically destructive sense. We must also consider the impact of the computer hacker who attacks networks and may cause great damage, perhaps financially or even from loss of time and data.

6. There will be less freedom of action. Someone will always be watching, listening, or reading. The ability to sense will exceed the ability to protect vital information. Information technologies will provide a wealth of information that can be used to conduct pattern analysis, review written communications (to include Internet traffic), and develop trends. What does this portend for the conduct of covert actions? For how long will a covert action remain out of the public eye? Electronic means will also provide instant access to events as they unfold. What does this transparency mean for the future of operations? Can we afford to engage in long, costly operations any longer?

7. There is a tenuous relationship between engagement and risk. Given the increased potential for viewing and dissecting each and every operation, engagement will take on a heightened level of risk. Engaging and losing will carry a greater risk than not engaging at all. Also, the very power that makes the United States a hyperpower makes the United States a target. Finally, it will be relatively easy to become engaged, but nearly impossible to disengage. These points argue for greater restraint before involving the United States in the affairs of other nations and perhaps a return to the Weinberger Criteria for ensuring that clear interests are at stake and that objectives are unambiguous.

8. Asymmetry in conflict will be the norm, not the exception. Given the overwhelming spending and capabilities of the United States, it will be difficult to find many potential adversaries that would be willing or even foolish enough to engage in a head-to-head conflict. Thinking more broadly about the nature of conflict, warfare is asymmetrical by nature. One side is always attempting to match its strengths against the other's weakness to gain an advantage. One area where potential Information Age foes will likely operate asymmetrically and have an advantage will be in the public domain in the war of ideas for the hearts and minds of populations.

9. The United States cannot have too many allies. Given the struggle for public approval, issues such as winning the information war and the competition for ideas will be based on the ability to build coalitions and establish legitimacy of operations. Allies will play an important role in the fight, not simply in terms of the capabilities they provide, but in their contributions to the ideological struggle. Failure to build diverse coalitions will have the tendency to cede the initiative to the enemy from the very beginning of an intervention or operation and expose vulnerable seams for the enemy or adversary to exploit. The antidote for this is broad multilateral support from the beginning.

10. There are some nations and alliances that may naturally threaten or prove predatory to the United States and its interests. Such is the case of the terrorists such as Osama bin Laden. In this case, the solution space or range of acceptable outcomes from the U.S. perspective can only be destruction of the threat. In severe cases, this will be the only course of action. For example, despite bin Laden's offer of a truce in January 2006, a settlement that would satisfy all parties is extremely unlikely given the great divergence in strategic objectives.

11. It's a matter of "when," not "if." With the proliferation of nuclear, biological, and chemical technologies for civilian use and the potential for incorporation of the same technologies for military or threatening purposes, it is reasonable to assume that at some point, weapons of mass destruction will be employed. The use of a chemical weapon on a Tokyo subway clearly demonstrates the potential for their use. Even the employment of conventional bombs on the Madrid and London subway systems provides ample evidence of the potential for more frequent and potentially more lethal attacks. Unfortunately the laws of probability and statistics are against us here, as a determined adversary, ready to die for a cause, will not likely be thwarted 100 percent of the time. Thus preparations for consequence management and mitigation will be imperative.

12. "It's the economy, stupid." Using a line from the Clinton-Gore campaign of 1992 as an illustration, the case is made that economics matter. A direct relationship exists between economic development, freedom and democracy, and large, unemployed, young populations. Where the leading economic indicators are positive, there is a high probability that societies will be democratic, unemployment rates low, and positive globalization trends emerging. Likewise where economic indicators are negative, wealth is unevenly distributed, and unemployment is high, there is a high probability that the negative aspects of globalization including instability and disenfranchisement of populations will be present.

Given these principles for the Information Age, what do they imply about requirements for the twenty-first-century leader? How should this leader determine what is important? How can a single person be expected to sort through so much information? Are there limits to the amount of data that the human mind can absorb in this new environment? And if so, what are the limits?

Unfortunately, if one makes the wrong choice, one is likely to spend time looking at trees rather than the forest. Consider the example of a congressional topic of interest, allegations of detainee abuse in Iraq and Afghanistan. Congress has spent significant time and effort examining this issue. Numerous hearings in 2004 and 2005 were held to establish the extent and cause of this horrible breach of conduct. Despite all the investigations that have been conducted, some in Congress continue to call for commissions to study the subject and potentially enact laws to set parameters on the treatment of prisoners of war, detainees, and others held in U.S. custody. While additional information may surface, the real issue becomes whether the additional information will be worth the investment in time and national capital. Perhaps it would be more useful to spend the scarce resources examining a topic of more strategic importance where legislation is clearly more appropriate, such as in the area of the use of the Reserve Component (RC) in the military. This issue centers around whether the paradigm and the laws concerning the use of the RC should be revised to reflect the real-world changes that have seen the RC go from a strategic reserve (only to be used in the case of national emergency) with a supporting role in homeland security to an operational rotation force (as used in Iraq beginning in 2003), a homeland defense force (as following the terrorist attacks of September 11, 2001), and a strategic reserve.

It is my firm belief that understanding the nature of the Information Age and the demands of globalization will become even more critical to the national security leader. Leaders must be trained and conditioned to make the right choices in spending our national security resources, including time available to the leader and the organization. As General Marshall said on the eve of World War II, "Years ago we had the time to prepare and no resources. Today we have the resources, but no time." We do not want to be in this position in the Information Age where the survival interests are likely to be just as great.

When people talk about national security and defense, the discussion inevitably turns to the question of military balance. Measuring concrete capabilities such as the number of weapons systems can be easily done. The result becomes a simple comparison of available hardware and tangible capabilities. How many tanks or aircraft does each side possess? Are the forces capable of projecting power and capability forward or are they merely a self-defense force tied to the owning nation?

Once the weapons systems comparison is complete, a likely follow-up discussion of quality ensues. In many instances, quality is related to the capabilities that are embedded in a piece of equipment based on software enhancements or advance technologies. These enhancements may impact the range of a weapon system or its accuracy. But in many cases, it is not so straightforward. For example, perhaps the quality is based on the ability to acquire targets or the lines of software code in the system. But even with both quantity and quality as measured in numbers of systems and their quality, the balance may not be clear. The more important question is, What does it really mean for the overall outcome of a particular strategy?

In fact, these calculations used to develop strategies and other leader calculations of this balance will not be sufficient in the Information Age. Given the increasing incorporation of information technologies into the tools of national security, more than a measure of simple military balance will be required.

In *Securing America's Future: National Strategy in the Information Age*, I present the need for a new National Security Act of 20XX.[1] The purpose of a new strategy would be to more effectively account for the transition that has occurred as the United States has moved into the Information Age and to more fully incorporate the elements of national power. The thesis is that a new strategy that fundamentally changes the *end, ways, means, risk,* and *environment* calculations must be developed.

Additionally, inherent in this new strategy is the need for a comprehensive reorganization of the U.S. government to allow for coordinated and rapid responses. Unfortunately the recent changes to our national security have had the effect of making changes to components of our security and defense capabilities in an isolated rather than coordinated manner.

Consider the establishment of the Department of Homeland Security (DHS) and the publication of a National Strategy Homeland Security (NSHS). This addition to the government and accompanying strategy in many regards compete with the Department of Defense and the National Security Strategy (NSS) that has been published since the mid-1980s. Effectively, this move has created a dangerous seam between foreign and domestic security and defense.

As further evidence of the difficulties of developing an integrated strategy one piece at a time is the creation of the Director of National Intelligence position, which gives the director of this new organization oversight and some budgetary authority still to be negotiated and evolved, over the sixteen different agencies in the Intelligence Community (IC). It is not that this authority is not needed, but somewhere between the concept and the execution needs to be a coherent plan of action.

The same can be said of the Department of State's efforts to set up a Stability and Reconstruction Office (SRO) to oversee the ability of the nation to conduct what has become know as Phase IV, post-conflict operations. The complexity of this developmental effort coupled with the requirement to cut across virtually all departments and agencies of the U.S. government clearly signals a need for coordination at a level higher than the State Department, such as the National Security Council (NSC).

A second theme is to broaden the manner in which we think about security and defense by incorporating environment into future strategic policy formulations. In this way the leader will gain a greater perspective of the overall situation and the cultural issues being faced.

All of this taken together suggests that the leader of the Information Age will have a broader set of requirements beyond the understanding of the traditional hard power elements of national power and will face a world of increasing threats and complexity. The twenty-first-century leader will need to have a more complete understanding of the total national capabilities available and learn to wield them in a way to maximize opportunities and avoid the risks.

As of 2006, the United States spends over half a trillion dollars on defense.[2] But how much goes toward training, education, and experiences for the Information Age leader? Examination of the DoD budget certainly does not indicate large expenditures in the development of leaders. Admittedly, the DoD has well-articulated systems of schools and education as well as a training system for individuals and complete unit training, but how are the requirements for developing Information Age leaders being infused into the force? Furthermore, how much of this total is spent on the leadership development and the essential transformation in leadership that must occur? More importantly, what changes in the leadership development within the other key security and defense contributors are occurring given the broadening of the concept of security and defense to go beyond the DoD? It would be insufficient to only make changes in the leadership as applied to the hard power elements without also implementing necessary changes in the soft power elements.

A Different Way of Thinking

In the Industrial Age, data flowed in hierarchical bands along well-defined chains of command or lines of authority. The information available to the leader was almost metered with the major issue being a lack of timely and accurate data on which to base decisions. Information also generally flowed in intervals. Reports were provided to leaders on a regular basis and scheduled feedback loops were embedded in organizations to provide updates. Few, if any, could ever be accused of having either timely or too much information. In fact, in many cases data provided to decision makers was often considered obsolete upon delivery.

Consider, for example, that in trying to get a jump on the markets, investment banks would send runners to meet the planes arriving from overseas in order to get the latest copies of the international newspapers that were, in the case of most of Europe, six hours ahead of the East Coast markets. The goal was always to speed up the feedback mechanisms to gain greater advantages in decision cycles. Today that same information is beamed worldwide in milliseconds immediately after it is published.

The same was true in national security where one was always waiting for the next satellite imagery and signals intelligence intercept. Regardless of the quality of data, it never seemed to be enough or on time. Consider the army's targeting system, which calls for a sequence of Observing, Detecting, Deciding, Delivering, and Assessing (ODDDA) for targeting. This is a very linear process in which targeting meetings are held on a cyclic basis and targets are nominated and developed within a predetermined timeline. In this system, targets are passed up hierarchical chains of command and assessed for their importance. The process is plodding and methodical, certainly not agile and flexible. To further illustrate the point, consider the air force's Air Tasking Order (ATO), which is published every twenty-four hours and provides the target assignments for all aircraft flying in theater during a prescribed period. One assignment change, and the day's ATO was rendered obsolete.

The Information Age will be vastly different, and therefore the demands on the leader will also change. Rather than having to fight for data and information as in the Industrial Age, in the Information Age, the data available will be overwhelming. The key will be to turn raw data into information and information into knowledge that can be acted upon to achieve stated goals and objectives, while denying this same access to adversaries. Data will flow anywhere and everywhere. The speed of the processor will have only marginal meaning as the hardware speeds will overmatch the human dimension. Stated explicitly, hardware, software, and firmware will prove overwhelming to the human biological processor and network.

The result will be that the next major revolutionary advances in IT will be in the growth and sophistication of decision support tools and knowledge management capabilities. These areas will demand more resources and attention to ensure retaining overmatch over potential foes. The real money will be in the development of systems and capabilities that allow for the mining of the right single critical piece of information out of the millions of data elements available, truly finding an electronic needle in a haystack.

Security fits nicely into the category of an area demanding increasingly more attention. We will need to deal with the cyber threats that are emerging and employ multilevel security schemes to ensure that information is available to the right people but denied to all others. Consider that information concerning the development of WMDs has been posted on the Web for all to access. There is enough information available to understand the production, employment, and effects of one of these weapons. The question in the future is how to police and discipline the Internet to eliminate proliferation of threats. Certainly related issues will include the question of whether today's laws and international agreements can support enforcing the breaches in security, intellectual property rights, or other difficult issues that are likely to arise in the Information Age.

Strategy in the Industrial Age has often been compared to a chess game. In thinking about the Cold War challenges, the example of an international chess match between the United States and the Soviet Union, and more broadly between the North Atlantic Treaty Organization (NATO) and the Warsaw Pact comes to mind. If this analogy holds, then in the Information Age, the analogy is a three-dimensional chess game with time limits for each move where only portions of the board are exposed at any one time while playing five simultaneous games. Managing the complexity of this competition will be challenging indeed. It will require learning to think in new dimensions. It will also mandate learning to live with and making decisions under conditions of intense ambiguity, something that few are comfortable doing.

Think about the adage that says that it is better to make a decision based on 90 percent of the information than to wait for 100 percent before making a decision. Imagine what would it be like to make the decision based on 80 percent, 60 percent, or even with less than 50 percent of the information available. This question brings a whole new meaning to the concept of risk.

One must also learn to master the transitions that will occur very rapidly in the execution of the grand strategy. These periods of transitions will present windows of opportunity that will open and close very rapidly. Failure to take advantage of the opportunity during these narrow windows may expose the United States and its allies to risk and potentially a threat to being able to achieve our national goals and objectives. Once an opportunity is lost, other opportunities may be few and far between.

In dealing with transitional periods, the nation and its leaders must learn to multitask and parallel process. An example from the military is the concept of conducting the "three-block war." This phrase was first used by the commandant of the U.S. Marine Corps, Gen. Charles Krulak, in the aftermath of operations in Somalia. The idea was that forces—and by extension the other government agencies participating with the military in an operation—needed to have the capability to operate in multiple types of operations in a nearly simultaneous manner. For example, in one block, humanitarian operations might be ongoing, perhaps delivering aid to the population. In the next block, operations might entail the separation of forces or peacekeeping to reestablish security and prevent further violence. In the third block, forces might be participating in combat operations to defeat an adversary. If this concept is not complex enough, the forces on the ground also need to have the ability to transition rapidly between operations, so the force involved in combat could very rapidly be expected to transition to a humanitarian operation immediately following termination of hostilities.

While the term "forces" has been used, we will need to think more broadly about what constitutes these units. It is likely that in the first block of this three-block war soldiers, contractors, state department officials, and city planners, as an example, will all be working in a coordinated manner to conduct nation-building operations. Finally, adding to the complexity is that in the Information Age, we must be able to conduct these operations and make these transitions with cameras rolling and live footage being beamed around the world, as in the case of operations in Iraq in March 2003 during Operation Iraqi Freedom.[3]

In this new way of thinking, the starting point, the development of requirements, and the steps to the objective will have a significant impact on reaching the right destination. Consider the development of a new family of tactical radios for the military, the Joint Tactical Radio System (JTRS). Since the introduction of the radio in World War I, each of the services have developed their own radio systems in various frequencies ranges for specific missions. Separate families of radios were developed for shorter-range communications in the higher bands using Frequency Modulated (FM) signals. Many of these systems could be found in ground units where the distances between units were measured in meters or kilometers. For longer-range communications, as for use in aircraft or ships, Amplitude Modulation (AM) systems tended to have greater utility. Of course, where aircrews needed to talk to soldiers on the ground, interface applications such as embedding liaison teams with ground forces allowed for passing the required information on targets, requirements for engaging targets, and the location of friendly forces. Most recently, there has been a significant growth in the proliferation of satellite systems for even longer-range and higher-capacity systems.

The initial idea behind the JTRS program was to replace the current variety of radio systems with a single platform that would have various computer-generated waveforms, including FM, AM, and satellite compatibility, as well as waveforms dedicated to high capacity data transmission. The concept appears to be sound; however, in practice it equates to improving upon current capabilities rather than thinking about the requirement holistically and working backward to develop a revolutionary new capability. Quite predictably, the development of this system is proceeding as an integrated joint service radio system. Assuming that the current programmatic issues can be solved, the system produced will be an evolutionary improvement in the current family of tactical radios—as of this writing, issues with cost, schedule, and performance abound.

In looking at the JTRS example, the issue with the system development lies as much in the question that was asked up front as much as in the complexity of the system to be developed. In fact the way one asks the question, in many regards, sets the stage for the answer and the eventual outcome; this was certainly true for the JTRS. Consider the subtle, yet important difference in asking, What system should be developed to replace the current fleet of military radios while providing a greater capacity for data throughput and networking? or What is the most effective and efficient manner of providing voice and data information throughout the battlespace?

The first question presupposes a solution that begins with the current radio and from that baseline builds a multimode, multifrequency enhanced system that performs very similarly to today's radio, albeit with significantly greater capability. Not a bad outcome, but certainly not a revolutionary capability either.

The second question allows for a new way to examine the problem. The basic idea is development of a system to provide a capability to communicate, without any constraint on the type of system to be considered. In fact, commercial technology already exists that allows for networking using Internet protocol (IP) solutions, sometimes also referred to as 802.X, using wireless connections. Consider the relative ease of developing a home network. For a modest investment, both hardwire and wireless networking is readily available with the ease of installation that allows even nontechnical people to establish 54 MBs throughput throughout one's home.

So instead of trying to develop another radio solution, the functionality of a radio could be developed using a purely IP-based solution. One might ask how to replicate the network structure of the radio that allows for all stations in the network to listen to the voice traffic. If you think about the capabilities to communicate through websites or in chat rooms that are normally done with data, and then expand that capability to include a voice over IP (VOIP) solution, you can begin to see the potential for an IP-based solution to the JTRS problem. A radio net with twenty stations could be replicated by having each individual station access a Web location with VOIP capabilities. Stations could enter and leave the net simply by clicking out of the window. By adding different transmission means such as the FM, AM, or satellite (and the proper antennas) with the required security equipment to encrypt the data, one can begin to see a unique solution to the JTRS problem.

In this case, it is unlikely that the old tried-and-true linear approach to problem solving will result in solutions that maximize the potential of this new era. Not to say that the only path to success will be the adoption of these state-of-the-art techniques and capabilities, but rather that the use of Information Age thinking will have the best chance to take advantage of the full opportunities and potential.

Network-Centric Operations

In the new Information Age national security environment, some of the most creative thought has come from the Office of Force Transformation within the Office of the Secretary of Defense. In a document titled "The Implementation of Network-Centric Warfare," the concepts that will begin to drive the environment and challenge leaders begin to emerge.[4] While the title implies that warfare is the focus, the discussion contained in the document is sufficiently broad to allow for the full range of thinking about network-centric operations, including the impact on the other non-military elements of power.

The network-centric concept in the Office of the Secretary of Defense construct postulates four domains: physical, information, cognitive, and social.[5] The domains are represented by four circles that have overlapping areas (see figure 1). The physical domain is the traditional domain of warfare, the physical space that can be easily measured in terms of numbers of systems, time, and distance. This is the primary domain in which we operated at the height of the Cold War. Most traditionalists in the field of national security would probably feel most comfortable in this domain.

The other three domains are considerably more difficult to measure or reduce to a scientific outcome. The information domain is "where information is created, manipulated, and shared," and the place where commander's intent and intelligence reside.[6] It is where one develops and disseminates a common operational picture of the world and begins to formulate an understanding of the environment. The cognitive domain is "in the mind of the warfighter." It includes the "intangibles of leadership, morale, unit cohesion, level of training and experience, and situational awareness," as well as "encompassing commander's intent, doctrine, tactics, techniques, and procedures." Finally, the social domain is "where humans interact, exchange information, form shared awareness and understandings, and make collaborative decisions. This is also the domain of culture, the set of values, attitudes, and beliefs held and conveyed by leaders to the society, whether military or civilian."

What is of the most interest in this formulation is that America has focused considerable resources on the physical domain, where battles are won or lost with overwhelming force and system superiority, but considerably less effort in the other domains in which wars are won or lost. In fairness, the United States has begun to recognize the importance of the other domains and has worked to expand its capabilities, but not to the same level.

Figure 1.
Information Age Warfare: Domains of Conflict

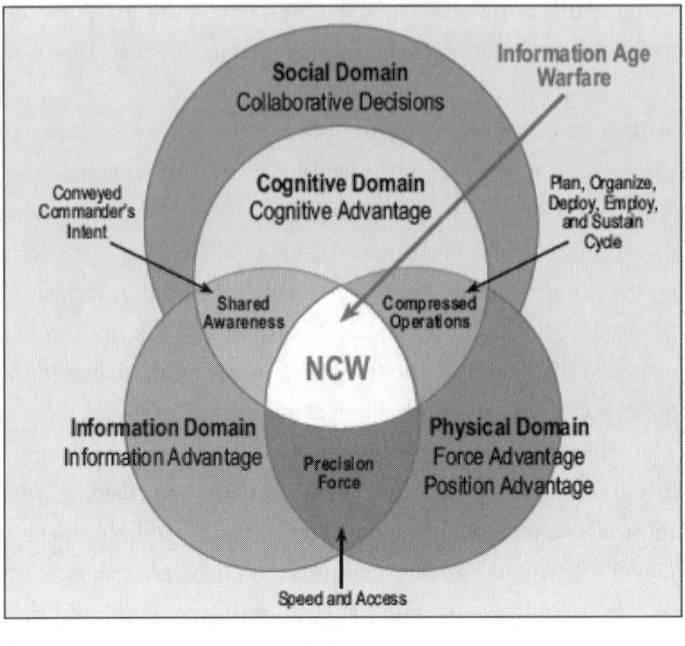

As an example, the U.S. military has developed training centers for teaching leaders how to deal with ambiguous situations and broadened the training to include the three-block war environment. Significant investments have been made in intelligence, surveillance, and reconnaissance (ISR) capabilities. Most recently, language and cultural sensitivity have been emphasized to a greater extent.

This "Domains of Conflict" concept has great importance for our discussion of the Information Age and the impact of this new era upon leaders and their organizations. The strategist or leader must gain an appreciation for and understanding of the competition that will be continuously waged in each of these domains. Furthermore, the strategist must be able to factor this into any realistic strategic assessments and plans. Winning in one domain does not ensure success in the overall campaign. Even winning in three out of the four domains may not be sufficient to assure a successful outcome.

In many ways, this framework assists in the understanding of asymmetric operations or warfare. If the United States becomes engaged in a war of ideas and attempts to respond with tools from the physical domain only, the potential for failing to meet the national goals and objectives is high. A strategy using tanks against ideas misses the point and will result in a less than optimal outcome for the side employing the tanks. If the United States has force and position advantage but the adversary has information advantage, nothing short of total annihilation would be able to trump the flow of ideas, assuming they involved the adversary's survival interests.

The intersections within the diagram are also relevant. Where the cognitive and information domains intersect is the intersection of the mind of the commander with information; at this point, a situational awareness is generated. This is where the commander begins to understand the battlespace and develop plans based on the *coup d'oeil* that Clausewitz described in *On War*. Where the information and physical domains intersect, the ability to generate precision force is produced. The degree to which absolute freedom of action is generated depends on the relative comparison of information and physical attributes. That is, only if one has necessary positional information, do the advantages of the precision of the weapons ensue; if information is lacking, all the precision capabilities in the world will not allow for successfully engaging the adversary. Finally, where the cognitive and physical domains intersect, the ability to operate in compressed timelines is generated: the ability to execute the decision cycle more rapidly than one's adversary. However, it is at the intersection of the four domains that the ability to conduct network-centric warfare, or operations in the case of the general-purpose national security leader, is generated. The greater efficiency in purpose is generated by bringing the four domains to the maximum overlap such that all four are synchronized.

If one considers the history of strategic thought and conflict, it becomes clear that much of the focus of our efforts has been and continues to be in the physical domain. The Cold War had a large component that dealt extensively in this domain, in addition to the broader ideological conflict that pitted democracy against communism. What is the balance of power? How many tanks, artillery, and fixed wing aircraft do NATO and the Warsaw Pact have that were capable of influencing the battle along the East-West German border? How quickly can reinforcements arrive at the battlefield?

Of course, the Cold War also had cognitive and social domain aspects as both sides competed for the support and strength of the neutral and non-aligned nations of the world. Competition waged throughout the world in countries such as Vietnam and Afghanistan where the United States and its allies sought to halt the spread of communism, while the Soviet Union and its satellites worked to increase their sphere of influence.

Both sides also looked to gain advantages in the cognitive domain. The Soviet Union developed a complex assessment tool that attempted to weigh all aspects of the balance to include the values of each side. By developing very detailed control measures, the Soviet Union hoped to gain a decision cycle advantage, which would swing the balance in their favor. The methodology was called Correlation of Forces and Means (COFM).

While competition in the four domains is not a new phenomenon, the tools available to states and nonstate actors significantly impact the ability of to interact in the four domains. Consider the relative ease with which a society with information technologies can organize a demonstration. Word of mouth and dissemination of flyers has been replaced by sending an email announcing a demonstration to one hundred of one's friends, each of whom sends it to one hundred friends, each of whom send it to one hundred more friends. Without too much trouble, we have just sent the demonstration announcement to one million people without even leaving the computer terminal.

The ability to proliferate ideas and disseminate information and disinformation in vast quantities has become ordinary. Once the information begins its journey, halting its flow or correcting misinformation becomes extremely difficult, sometimes impossible. It is similar to the flow of a computer virus, watching data travel around the world to have a near simultaneous delivery at hundreds of disparate points. At one point after 9/11, there was a theory that the Pentagon, on 9/11, was hit not by a plane controlled by terrorists, but rather by a stray U.S. missile intending to take down one of the airliners. In a single day, the details of this assertion were sent to me by nine different people complete with a PowerPoint brief making this argument.

For actors with limited ability to operate in the physical domain, the only alternative is to operate in the other three, where they may indeed have an advantage. Competitors that lack strength in the physical domain because of poor-quality or a lack of equipment will likely attempt to compete against the United States in a war of ideas, information, or public opinion where they are more likely to have parity or even an advantage.

The adversaies we are facing in Baghdad in Operation Iraqi Freedom (whether one considers them to be terrorists, former regime elements, or enemy combatants) that began attacking U.S. forces in 2003 with roadside bombs certainly cannot compete with the military might of Coalition forces, and so the insurgents attempt to limit direct confrontation except for specific purposes at a time and place of their choosing. But this same adversary potentially has an advantage in the social and information domains and perhaps even in the cognitive domain, since the initiative for attacks generally rests with the adversary in this conflict. The result is the tug-of-war for the hearts and minds of the Iraqi people that has been raging since the formation of the insurgency in mid-2003.

In this contest, the insurgents work to convince the Iraqi people that the Coalition forces should withdraw, describing the conflict as a confrontation between the West and Islam, while the Coalition attempts to make the case that Iraqis are better off today with Saddam Hussein's ousting and the demise of the Baathist regime. In the middle is the average Iraqi who would like to have basic services, such as running water, electricity, trash removal, and a working sewage system.

What complicates the merging of the domains and prevents operating in the center of the diagram in the network-centric area is that aside from the physical domain, which is primarily comprised of the military from within the Department of Defense, the other domains are largely shared throughout the U.S. government, and in some cases reside outside of the government's sphere of influence. For example, in the social domain, the Department of State, the U.S. Agency for International Development (USAID), the media, nongovernmental organizations (NGOs), society or the public (both ours and those of the other parties involved), and even religious organizations play an important role. Imagine trying to align the attitudes and opinions of all of these organizations on any single outcome.

This idea of competing in the non-physical domains will become even more important for success in this new era, and fortunately this concept is beginning to be better understood. I recently heard a senior DoD leader say that the most important shot fired in the global war against extremism was the deployment of the mobile army surgical hospital (MASH) into Pakistan to provide relief to survivors following the devastating earthquake in 2005 that killed perhaps eighty thousand people and left hundreds of thousands homeless. Being able to interact productively by providing much needed medical supplies and humanitarian relief demonstrated U.S. goodwill and caring to the people of Pakistan and the global Islamic community. This interaction in the social domain came at a time when most of the U.S. dialogue with the Islamic world was perceived to be in the physical domain with the use of force, thus improving the perception of the United States abroad.

In the Information Age, the successful leader will be one who can move back and forth within the domains rapidly and develop coherent plans to address the various permutations in this "Rubik's cube" environment. In this complex environment, little leeway to the left or right is acceptable; one wrong move, and potentially all the progress made can be wiped out. Going back to the example of the earthquake in Pakistan, much of the goodwill generated by the support rendered to the Pakistani people in the aftermath of the disaster was dissipated by the killing several months later of seventeen Pakistanis (including several intended targets) by a missile fired from a Predator unmanned aircraft engaging al Qaeda leadership targets. The killings resulted in demonstrations and violence directed at the United States and the government of Pakistan, President Pervez Musharraf in particular. The question for our leaders is whether the public relations aftermath was worth the killing of a handful of terrorist leaders. Did we win or lose this engagement in the information and social domains? And perhaps more important, what impact will this have on the overall war against violent extremism?

A New Way to Lead

In the Information Age, leadership by attraction will begin to replace leadership by direction. The analogy is "soft power" versus "hard power" in directing the efforts of people and organizations in this new age. The ability to motivate, convince, and cause a synergy between people of similar ideas and goals will begin to replace the more coercive, direct, and compelling leadership style. The free flow of information will have the result of allowing people to better understand their environment, conditions, options, and opportunities to act in their perceived self-interest.

For military commanders, this translates to less ability to control the individual actions of all subordinates within the command, yet through enhanced information flow and force capabilities, a greater capacity for decisive engagements with great effect by individual operators. Additionally, the dispersal of formations and operators across vast spaces will provide an unprecedented opportunity to execute according to their personal discretion. Even if commanders wanted to micromanage the actions of subordinates, the technologies available to the individual soldier would prevent this sort of over-managed direction.

So where in the Industrial Age, mass and strength were the coin of the realm, in the Information Age, ideas and attraction will take on new and growing importance. The Information Age leader will still have to master the mechanical part of leading large organizations such as getting the right people, organizations, or forces (as in the case of the military), and support to the right place at the right time. But this is really more about the control portion of Command and Control (C2), the part that assists leaders and commanders with implementing directives and setting the conditions for mission success.

The commander must also exercise mastery of the command portion of C2. Therefore, the question really becomes, if leadership in the Information Age is becoming more about the conveyance of ideas than the issuing of orders, what changes must the leader make to be successful?

First and foremost, the leader's ability to accurately and completely articulate intent to all personnel within the organization becomes paramount. Intent relates to what missions need to be accomplished, what the limits and authorities are for those executing the missions, and what the required endstate is. If any one of these points is not understood to the level at which the execution of the operation is occurring, then the outcome is in jeopardy. A soldier or airman that attacks a civilian target and causes considerable collateral damage at a critical point when the United States is trying to build ties between the American forces and the civilian population will likely do considerable damage to the operation and increase the time needed to regain the favor of the population.

Leaders of the Information Age must have the ability to develop and communicate concepts that translate into the execution by organizations and individuals to achieve desired objectives using the appropriate policies and strategies. This concept, discussed frequently as one of the principles of war, is known as unity of effort.[7] This may not sound like a new idea, but what the Information Age has done, which is unique as compared to the Industrial Age, is to compress time, expand distances, add orders of magnitude in terms of precision, and allow individuals to have an impact that heretofore even large organizations have been unable to achieve.

This inversion is interesting because in many respects both the theater commander and the individual foot soldier have the capability to have a strategic impact. Commanders receive training, education, and experiences that presumably prepare them for these strategic decisions. For example, in the case of a theater commander with over 100,000 personnel assigned, over thirty years of preparation have gone into building the leadership skills and conceptual understanding of operations. In the case of the individual soldier, the preparation period could be a short as several months of training. How can we possibly expect the same level of strategic thought in both senior commander and the soldier? Furthermore, how can we offset this lack of strategic insight of the soldier by introducing measures or controls, or even limiting capabilities?

Along with the concept of balancing control measures with the freedom of action is the inherent concern that "over-control" can have significant consequences just as "under control." A plan that is overly directive and fails to allow for opportunities that present themselves during execution will in all likelihood put the mission at just as great a risk as a fluid plan. Certainly it can put individual soldiers at risk; consider a set of rules of engagement (ROE) that is overly restrictive, which could lead to hesitation at the point of action. An individual may fail to act on instinct and thus provide the adversary a window to begin the engagement first resulting in friendly casualties. This is where the concept of commander's intent becomes critical.

In the military, the commander's intent is defined as specifying the purpose, method, and endstate of a particular operation, whether in combat, peacekeeping, or humanitarian operations. The purpose refers to the stated goal. What is to be achieved? The method specifies how the commander intends to have the purpose achieved. Finally, the endstate is a clear description of the outcome of the operation. For example, Coalition forces will deliver humanitarian supplies to the people of Kosovo (purpose) using air and ground transportation over a ninety-six-hour period while ensuring the security of the support centers and coalition forces using the minimum necessary force (method) to alleviate the human suffering and allow for NGO support to arrive (endstate).

I would argue that the commander's intent becomes more critical as operations become more dispersed and execution is at lower levels of command. In the Napoleonic phalanx, the individual soldier knowing the commander's intent seems considerably less important when the key for this soldier was to hold the lines and keep men to his left or right. On the other hand, the soldier of today operating as part of a fire team or squad needs to be able to pick up with the mission and execute commander's intent even in the event of the immediate leader becoming a casualty. In short, the altered time and space relationships greatly increase the importance of commander's intent.

To carry the argument even further, in the Clausewitz discussion of leadership, the concept of *coup d'oeil* was used to describe the commander's ability to see and understand the battlespace. Given the expectation that execution of key operations will take place at lower levels and the increased autonomy of lower level formations, *coup d'oeil* must be resident at lower and lower levels of command, maybe even at the individual soldier's level.

The Geometry of Leadership

The Industrial Age saw the development of well-defined hierarchical structures for organizations including for command and control of military forces. Theories abound concerning the limits of an individual to exercise necessary authority and direction over subordinates. For example, in the military, the generally accepted principle was that a single commander could effectively command and control three to five subordinate organizations. These limits were based largely on the ability to effectively communicate between levels of command, including passing data and instructions up and down established hierarchical chains of command. Other studies have concluded that five to nine is the more typical limit. Of course the field or situation under which leader is operating also affects the discussion of the theoretical span of control.

This structure resulted in an organization that resembled a pyramid, with discrete communications between hierarchical levels. Commanders generally talked to other commanders, operations officers to other operations officers, and intelligence officers to other intelligence officers. A majority of the integration was done horizontally, say at the division, where inputs from the brigades and guidance from the corps allowed the division staff to assemble a plan. So once all of the division staff officers had collected their data from higher and lower elements, the synchronization of their level of command was possible.

Therefore the organizations that developed adhered in large measure to these informal rules with the result that a 17,000-soldier army division had three maneuver brigades and the requisite support to control a linear frontage of thirty or forty kilometers. The division's higher headquarters, the corps, thus had the doctrinal requirement to command and control three to five divisions as subordinate elements.

Examining the flow of information in these nested formations provides great insight into how planning and operations were conducted. Orders were passed from higher headquarters following an intensive mission analysis that allowed the senior commander to take one third of the available time prior to execution. As each higher-level commander performed this same ritual, the time available at the platoon level (which is subordinate to a company, battalion, brigade, division, and corps) was minimal. This deliberate planning process leaves the lowest levels, which will eventually be required to execute the operation, with little time to plan, rehearse, and stage prior to the execution.

While the example above uses the military chain of command to illustrate the hierarchical nature of operations, this formulation was not restricted to the military. The interagency process, developed with the passing of the National Security Act of 1947, established a National Security Council chaired by the president and consisting of the vice president, secretary of state, and secretary of defense; additionally, the 1947 act created the process for deliberating national security issues. The term "interagency" refers to the grouping of departments, organizations, and agencies within the U.S. government that cooperate and coordinate national policy. Members of the interagency deliberations on a particular issue vary on a case by case basis, and the grouping can be expanded in an ad hoc fashion to include other nongovernmental organizations and agencies that may be called upon to provide input on matters of special interest or to coordinate for a specific purpose. The coordination of efforts is supervised by the National Security Council (NSC). Interagency deliberations normally proceed from the working group to the deputies committee to the principals' level, which includes the president, vice president, and cabinet-level secretaries. The results of deliberations or decisions are passed between the levels as coordination is conducted and decisions reached.

Both the military decision-making process and the interagency process described above are plodding and methodical formulations that allow for, and even demand, organized and hierarchical information flow. In both cases, the intent was to pass information up chains of command and then pass decisions down as necessary. While it was possible in both types of process to skip levels, the normal procedures called for a controlled and linear flow of information.

What changes to the structure of the national security system must be incorporated? And what changes to the information flow are necessary to support a new Information Age structure?

Clearly standing structures capable of immediate action are necessary. Whether we acknowledge it or not, we are in the early stages of conflict today with a number of different countries around the world engaging in information operations, global posturing, and in some cases open challenges, as in the case of Venezuela in 2005. Given the manner and rapidity with which strategic windows of opportunity will open and close, we must have all the necessary assets to react immediately.

Furthermore, our leaders must be trained and ready today as well. It will not be sufficient to become engaged in more than vigorous competition between states with no ability to respond.

The Moral-Ethical Dimension

The Information Age will have a dramatic impact on the moral-ethical aspects of leadership, command, the execution of missions, and accomplishment of objectives. Given the pervasiveness of digital audio-visual data and even the written word, the expectation of privacy and discretion is nearly unrealistic. Few operations, even those intended to be covert, will be able to remain out of the public domain for very long.

Each application of national security can and will be judged, and the method of judgment will not be always fair and just. Images seen through camera lenses may be taken out of context and fail to convey the truth about an incident. Unfortunately, once an image is in the public domain, providing the proper context will be nearly impossible.

Even the initial decisions on the situation, strategies to be employed, or the actual operations will be dissected. Strategic leaders as well as those on the ground executing the missions will be subject to ever-increasing accountability. Some will be judged rapidly and unfairly in an effort to ensure that confidence in the operation remains high in the public's eye.

We must also be prepared to accept that the public and potential adversary's calls for responsibility for real or envisioned misdeeds will receive scrutiny, even if not justified.

With news cycles down to minutes and hours, events of the day will be examined nearly continuously. In World War II, news traveled from the war zone by mail. Accounts of events, even key battles, were history by the time they were viewed and digested by the public. In contrast, today's battles are waged in faraway lands and beamed real-time into the living rooms of Americans—as well as the coffee houses and meeting places of our adversaries.

While we teach our soldiers about the Laws of Land Warfare, better known as the Hague and Geneva Conventions, our adversaries will operate in future battlefields with little or no regard for these "artificialities" of civilized warfare. Consider the case of Somalia in 1993 where the corpses of Americans were dragged through the streets in celebration.

Sometimes despite best intentions, violations of these conventions by Americans may occur, as in the case of the Abu Ghraib detainee abuse scandal that began in summer of 2003 and first surfaced publicly in January 2004. The scandal continued to receive front-page media scrutiny in 2006, over two years after the allegations were first made public. The damage done in the informational and social domains as a result of Abu Ghraib and other allegations of detainee abuse have left a lasting scar on the American image that is unlikely to be forgotten in the Islamic world for quite some time.

Unfortunately, winning the moral-ethical dimension in conflict will be based as much on perception as on reality, thus complicating the ability to dominate in the arena. The discussion of the social domain, where concepts such as culture, values, attitudes, and beliefs reside, relates well to this moral-ethical dimension; it is why events can be viewed and interpreted by different parties in such different ways.

Consider the incident in 2001 when a Chinese fighter aircraft bumped a U.S. reconnaissance aircraft in flight, damaging to the U.S. aircraft and causing the Chinese fighter to ditch into the water, killing the pilot. The interpretation of events by China and the United States was vastly different, due at least in part to the moral-ethical question of whether the U.S.

aircraft was encroaching into sovereign Chinese airspace or whether the U.S. aircraft was operating appropriately in international airspace. The Chinese pilot was hailed as a hero defending the homeland by the Chinese, while in America the incident was largely covered as an unprovoked act of aggression by China.

This same sort of moral-ethical lens can be used to interpret the various responses to the events of 9/11 throughout the world. In many Islamic nations, despite the overwhelming condemnation by the governments, many individuals expressed support or at least some understanding of why these terrorists' acts were perpetrated.

The Information Age strategists and leaders must be prepared to deal with these ambiguities and have appropriate countermeasures and responses to negate these sorts of issues.

Leaders as Learning Organisms

An important key to success in the Information Age will be the ability to master the decision cycle and make necessary changes more rapidly than the adversary or the potential threat. Inherent in gaining the advantage in this area will be to have plans and doctrine developed and in place to allow for rapidly executing operations and seizing the initiative. Since, as the old military adage says, "no plan survives first contact," each leader and organization must have systems readily available to provide immediate feedback, facilitate assessments, develop changes to existing plans, and disseminate the changes to the organizations and leaders that will execute the updated plans.

Leaders and their organizations must also have flexibility, adaptability, and versatility.[8] Flexibility pertains to being able to respond to new, different, or changing requirements. Adaptability allows for modification according to changing circumstances. Versatility implies having many uses or applications. While the three terms are closely related, subtle differences exist. For example, when an organization plans to execute an operation at a certain time, but has the execution sequence moved up, yet is still able to successfully complete the mission, it has demonstrated flexibility. In contrast, an organization that can modify its tactics, techniques, and procedures in response to the emerging situation in real time would be considered to be highly adaptable, while an organization able to conduct multiple missions such as combat, peacekeeping, or humanitarian operations would be considered versatile.

Many of these skills can be learned by leaders and organizations. Certainly the basic design of an organization has an impact on the degree to which units can display these characteristics, but leader and organizational initiative also plays a vital role. A leader that develops a single plan with a discrete outcome is likely to be surprised every time, while a leader that plans for branches and sequels based on possible situations that may arise is likely to have anticipated uncertainty and thus feels comfortable rapidly responding to changes in the environment.

This sort of flexibility must be incorporated into training as well so that the organization and subordinate leaders have the same degree of comfort as the developer of the plan. If it is true that "the enemy gets a vote," as many national security and uniformed military leaders like to say, then planning for changing situations makes prudent sense.

Consider the example of operations in Haiti in 1994 where the United States had developed two distinct plans to restore the legitimate Haitian government. The first plan called for the overthrow of the coup leaders using military forces, which would conduct a rapid takedown of the coup leaders' command and control apparatus and security forces using air, ground, and naval forces to overwhelm and seize control of Haiti. In the second plan, the assumption was that the coup leaders would voluntarily depart. In both plans the follow-on operation called for an interagency task force to arrive with the necessary capabilities to restore order, reestablish legitimate government control, and begin rebuilding the country. While most believed that the first plan was the most likely to be executed, planning for the second method of entry occurred and in fact it was the course of action implemented after former President Carter and Gen. Colin Powell brokered a deal for the coup leaders to be transported out of Haiti.

The twenty-first-century leader will find it necessary to plan for success as well as failure. A criticism of the plan for the invasion of Iraq in 2003 is that the plan failed to plan for success—senior political and military leaders did not anticipate a rapid overthrow of the Hussein regime and did not have the required follow-on forces capable of nation-building and other post-combat stability operations. In this operation, the lightning-fast blitz to Baghdad potentially contributed to the instability in the post-combat phase. Perhaps a question that will continue to haunt U.S. planners is whether better planning for these operations would have resulted in a vastly different Iraq in the post-combat phase and even years down the road. If the United States intends to conduct complex nation-building operations such as those in Bosnia, Kosovo, Afghanistan, and Iraq, then what changes to the national security strategy and organizations must occur to allow for a reasonable expectation of success?

A related debate that normally ensues when discussing strategic operations concerns the issue of command versus control. The topic of command and control has already been introduced as it pertains to span of control, but in this section, the question of commanding versus controlling is presented. In thinking about command and control, command generally is thought to be the art, while control pertains to the science. Thus in formulations of command and control, many attribute the art to the commander while relegating the science piece to the staffs. While the basic tenets of this logic will likely continue to hold, the successful Information Age leader will need to have greater ability to command with less constricting control measures to allow for taking advantage of opportunities, responding to challenges, and maximizing the potential of subordinate organizations.

This shifting in the weight of command versus control toward command will facilitate true learning by leaders and organizations. But the implications for more art and less science are also significant, and will affect the manner in which we train leaders. Of course trying to "train" someone in art will have its own set of challenges. If one subscribes to the notion that we train for certainty and educate for uncertainty, then the logical conclusion will be to weigh development over education and experience over training and drills.

The Information Age National Security Leader

The problem with defining the requirements that will be levied on the Information Age national security leader is that in a sense there is little good news. Simply stated, more will be demanded of this new age leader.

The old methods of leadership and providing direction will remain highly relevant, but this twenty-first-century leader will also have to master an increased pace, greater density of information, and greater scrutiny, among other new challenges.

Perhaps the first relevant question is who are the national security leaders that will shoulder this increased burden? The formal leaders established by the Constitution will undoubtedly have to be concerned with these new requirements.

The president, according to the Constitution, has a central role in the realm of national security and defense.[9] He serves as commander in chief of the armed forces and through legislation added in the aftermath of World War II makes significant use of the NSC, created by the National Security Act of 1947, along with the Central Intelligence Agency and the Department of the Air Force.

The president also has a large executive branch with responsibilities that cut across all of the elements of national power with the ability to gather information, develop policies, enforce standards, and conduct compliance checks. In structure and action, the executive branch is organized and functions as a large pyramid. Cross-leveling or sharing of information is done in a variety of ways. Daily interactions among departments and from departments to the president occur on an issue-by-issue basis. More information sharing is occurring as a result of some of the organizational changes that have occurred in the aftermath of 9/11 (e.g., between the DoD and the Department of Homeland Security). Interagency meetings conducted by NSC staff at lower levels or the president at a meeting of the full NSC also occur on an as-needed basis.

Information flows up and down the chain of command with stops at discrete points for consolidation and the development of positions on issues. Consider the case of intelligence support for operations in Iraq in which intelligence feeds from across the government were collected and utilized by the CIA to develop an assessment of the likelihood that Iraq had WMDs. At some level within the organization, the data was interpreted, an assessment made, and a briefing prepared for the president. This example highlights that even in a rote system such as this, mistakes can and will be made. Thus, an additional task for the Information Age leader will be to work to eliminate the causes of analytical mistakes and get the right information for use in making a timely and accurate assessment and decision.

The interagency process is deliberative and collaborative in many respects as a policy development entity, but certainly has little if any capability to conduct operations. In fact, neither the NSC nor the supporting staff has the inherent capabilities required of an operational headquarters or command. Thus a particular failing of the current system is that the president lacks the capability to conduct much other than a military response. Only the military has the organization, equipment, and command hierarchy to conduct operations. Certainly one could argue that other departments and agencies can contribute to and conduct limited operations. For example, the State Department can operate through the ambassadors as they pass information to and from host countries. The organization and agencies of the Intelligence Community can also act on presidential orders to collect information, conduct covert operations or conduct assessments, but they too have limited operational capability, usually for short-duration missions and tasks.

Congress also has formal and vital roles in the realm of security and defense.[10] The Constitution empowers Congress in particular to provide for the common defense and general welfare of the United States, to declare war, to raise and support an army, to provide and maintain a navy, to make rules for the government and regulation of the land and naval forces, and to raise a militia (National Guard).

So the question is not whether Congress has a role to play in this area, but is it suited by organizational structure to fulfill this role? If information sharing within the administration is challenged, then information sharing between the executive and legislative branches is sporadic and intermittent at best.

In contrast to the executive branch with the president in charge, Congress has 535 executives that must cooperate, reach consensus, and negotiate with the executive branch. The current system of collaboration is largely reduced to a "pull" system where Congress asks questions, conducts hearings, or convenes commissions to obtain information about security and defense issues. A system of scheduled formal deliberations, mostly dealing with the development and funding of budgets, is in place, but on questions of strategy or operations, it is largely à la carte.

To gain additional information, Congress has written into law such requirements as the Quadrennial Defense Review (QDR) and National Security Strategy (NSS) that mandate that the Department of Defense and the White House, respectively, submit periodic updates on security and strategy issues. While these documents are good reference materials, they cannot take the place of real-time collaboration in security and defense that is implied by the Constitutional language.

Even when debate occurs on a real-time basis, it appears most recently to be focused at the wrong level. Much of the security debate within Congress has tended to flock to tactical issues, such as whether individual soldiers have adequate armor protection or delivery schedules and distribution schemes for combat vehicles, rather than more strategic questions, such as the budget allocated among the ground, air, sea, space, and special operations forces. The first set of issues is certainly important and deserves to be addressed, but becoming the focus of congressional debate tends to result in myopia that misses the broader perspective. Rather, it is the second set of issues that deserves a clear vetting outside the political debate.

The role of the judicial branch in security and defense is less overt, yet still important.[11] The requirement for real-time deliberations in areas of security and defense is not necessary in most regards, and the Supreme Court has more of a deliberative, rather than operational, nature. Ruling on issues such as the treatment of detainees or the legalities of the Patriot Act are issues that fall under the purview of the judicial branch.

I would make the case in regard to the judicial branch that its role will need to greatly expand as we continue the national debate about the legalities of domestic spying and what some see as the erosion of individual rights in the aftermath of 9/11. More broadly, I do not believe that 9/11 is the cause for reexamining these fundamental issues. It was merely the catalyst. Globalization and the emergence of the Information Age mandate a reevaluation of certain principles. The Founding Fathers certainly could not have foreseen the technological enhancements that facilitate the diminishing of privacy. Additionally, it would be interesting to see how they would have balanced the right to privacy with the inherent responsibility of the government to secure its people given global threats that can penetrate an individual's property such as in a cyber attack on a personal computer or the spread of a deadly chemical cloud.

The role of state and local governments in security and defense issues has grown rapidly since 9/11 with little reason to believe that this trend will not continue. It would be difficult to find too many roles in state and local government that have not seen requirements created or expanded. Local police and firefighters must now be versed in dealing with mass casualty operations or at least understand how and where to get additional resources should they be overwhelmed. First responders must also be trained to recognize and report chemical or biological threats. New requirements for communications systems that allow for interface at the state and local levels as well as with federal authorities continue to increase.

Consider the new tasks of the city planner. The role has expanded to include questions such as standoff requirements for municipal buildings and capability to withstand bomb blasts or provide air filtration systems. The city planner must also consider the appropriate positions of cameras and ingress and egress routes. Even individual builders have a role to play in new construction and renovation of existing structures to ensure greater resilience and survivability. Decisions made in the design of structures from houses to buildings to stadiums can have a significant impact on whether people survive a manmade or natural disaster.

To be effective in these new roles, state and local officials need to have better training, systems that allow for real-time interface, and data links both up and down the chain of command. Information from national sources needs to be able to be filtered down to the appropriate levels where security and protection measures can be put in place. Obviously there are issues with protecting sources and means for sensitive information, but there are also issues with lower levels being able to make use of the data that is provided. How should training be changed within state and local governments to maximize the response capabilities?

At the same time, some of the best information may come from the lower levels where officials and even private citizens are seeing and reporting anomalies, such as the government official that sees a suspicious individual applying for release of sensitive material like a building plan or for a license for working as a crop duster. These should be triggers that cause the official to submit a report that can be correlated against other inputs and potentially thwart an attack.

In this new security environment, even civilian managers must be trained to act with security in mind. The local communications or cable operator who sees some strange inputs into his or her computer screen must be trained to be watchful, respond quickly, and report all security issues. Perhaps the operator is seeing the early stages of an electronic attack against U.S. infrastructure. The plant manager as well as the office manager must have plans in place in the event of a catastrophic attack. And it is not just the formal leaders that have a role to play in this new environment. Even the average citizen going about daily business must be aware of surroundings.

What this says for leaders is that regardless of one's "normal" tasks, such as supervising a car manufacturing plant, managing an industrial farm, working in the federal government in the Department of Homeland Security, or managing port operations in Baltimore, these leaders also have a role in security and defense. The times when security and defense were thought to be the sole ownership of only the thin crust of national leaders, the intelligence services, and the military are long gone. The ability in this globalized, highly interconnected world for threats to reach out and touch well into America's heartland translates to a new mandate for each person to his or her part to identify, report, and respond to suspicious situations.

I strongly believe that the Information Age signifies an important transition point for America in many regards, most especially in the areas of security and defense. If nothing else, 9/11 should have served as a wake-up call that the strategic pause following the Cold War was over and that the defense dividend that many budgeters had contemplated would not materialize.

The combination of globalization fueled by proliferation of information technologies has ushered in a new and potentially dangerous world. In this new environment of the Information Age, the ways and means of thinking about strategy need to be expanded to account for the new requirements levied upon the twenty-first-century leader.

In the next chapter, I will examine four important requirements for leaders and leadership in the Information Age. Leadership in this new age will be more demanding and complex. It is not that leaders will need to discard the basic tenets of leadership, but rather that their individual responsibilities and personal capabilities will need to expand greatly.

CHAPTER 4

Leading in the Information Age

Successful leadership in the Information Age will require the development of greater expertise in four key areas and place increasing demands on the twenty-first-century leader. This is not meant to imply that the body of knowledge concerning leadership in national security has been made irrelevant with the coming of the Information Age, but rather to demonstrate that key differences exist that call for corresponding changes in our concept and application of leadership. The four areas are (1) vision and communication, (2) analysis and judgment, (3) perspective, and (4) the three Is—imagination, innovation, and initiative.

Leadership has and will continue to become more rather than less complex. The tried-and-true methods and theories remain relevant, but must be augmented with new and improved concepts for dealing with a highly globalized, interconnected world.

First among equals are vision and communication—these two attributes sit at the apex of the pyramid, which rests on this firm foundation, representing the body of thought and knowledge concerning leaders and leadership. Vision and communication are equally supported and balance at the intersection of three foundational supports: analysis and judgment, perspective, and the three Is.

Figure 2.
Information Age Leadership

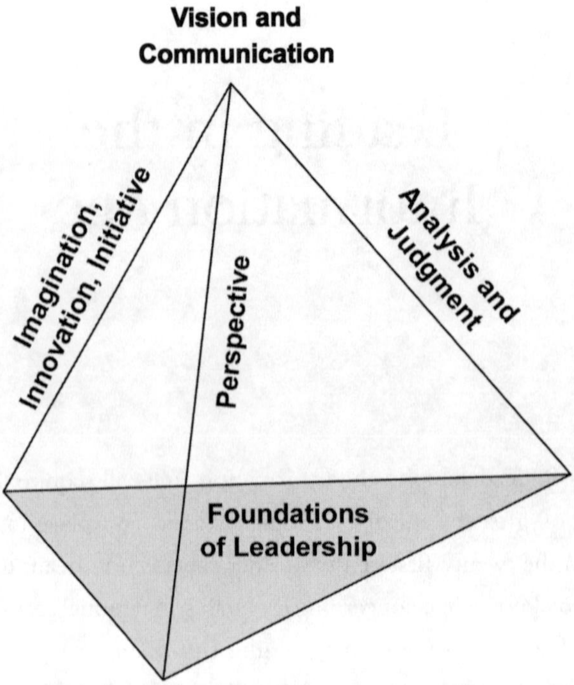

Vision and Communication

This section examines the concept of *vision* and *communication*. The two terms are inextricably linked as a vision for a leader and an organization will only be viable if it is communicated fully to the appropriate level where the execution occurs. Stated another way, a vision without communication is hallucination, while communication without a vision is simply noise.

Clearly the term "vision" means different things to different people. In one sense it is related to the ability to see. A medical doctor talking about the vision of a patient discusses the term in a very clear and precise manner: the patient has 20/20 vision or has an astigmatism that must be corrected, or the patient has cataracts that require surgery to restore vision. This is vision in the physical sense. It is easy to define and quantify.

The term may also be used in a supernatural or spiritual sense. The fortuneteller or prophet might speak of having a vision of a future event. Perhaps the vision in this sense is an impending disaster or prognostications concerning future fortunes. However, vision in the context of leadership examines the term as it relates to direction or focus for individuals or organizations in the pursuit of excellence.

This discussion is not intended to be a definitive articulation of the planning process, but rather a thought-provoking analysis that highlights the importance of having a plan or vision for the future. The concepts discussed in this section are not narrowly focused on a single segment of society, but rather designed to be a broad examination of the need for direction for individuals as well as leaders and managers.

The leader must have and impart a vision to exercise his or her leadership role within an organization in the pursuit of a stated outcome. The leader must not only instill in the organization a sense of direction, but also impart the creative impetus, the enthusiasm, and the firm hand when necessary to ensure organizational success.

Vision

In all aspects of daily life, one must have a direction or focus. I make this assertion from the beginning and will make the case that direction in all living things is imperative for accomplishing goals, including the basic need for survival.

The skeptic will immediately say that it is possible to survive without having any daily direction. He may claim to wake up and go from one activity to the other with no thought process or goal. Perhaps there is an element of truth to his statement; however, in the purest sense, the direction or goal becomes the physical act of getting up each morning and surviving another day. So there is direction, no matter how elementary.

Even insects such as honeybees have a direction. Perhaps to call it a vision is too strong, but it is clear that the bees in a hive work together in a single unit in order to accomplish a specific goal. They build their nest, all purposefully working together. They fly from flower to flower drawing out the pollen for sustenance. This purpose includes self-defense and defense of their environment as they work together to protect the queen bee, the leader of their individual nests. They have a clear sense of purpose.

Some will perk up quickly at the talk of direction or vision and are anxious to share their experiences about their goals. They speak of their vision as though it were an out of control freight train moving down the tracks at breakneck speeds, covering the course in record time. They move rapidly across the game board but miss the key milestones that help to define their direction. They might get there eventually, but they are unsure of where "there" is. Even when they get to a reasonable endstate[1], they will not be assured they will recognize it as a key goal or waypoint.

One must ask the hard questions. Is vision only something that great leaders have? Does having a vision pertain to individuals as well as organizations? Is it possible to be successful without having a vision?

What is the key to vision? Simply put, an effective vision must have a focus (or singleness of purpose) combined with energy and consistency in execution. The illustration of this point will be made with the following story.

The Farmer and His Sons

Once upon a time there was a farmer who had four sons: *Simple*, *Dreamer*, *Jumpy*, and *Wally*. The farmer worked the land diligently. He focused his energies on growing produce and had not branched out into raising farm livestock, although he always thought that the capability existed, given the size and attributes of the farm. Furthermore, he had taught each of his sons the methods of tilling the soil, harvesting the crops, and selling the produce.

The sons had equal training and were similar in size and physical capability. In fact, the only perceivable difference in the four sons was in the way they approached their goals and aspirations. *Simple* was content to exist from day to day, *Dreamer* had great ideas and boundless energy, *Jumpy* was always moving from one project to the next, and *Wally* was steady and sure.

Over the years, the family farm had grown to quite a large organization and had a number of workers that helped the farmer and his sons manage the business. Day after day, the loyal employees would report to work. They each had a great deal of experience working on the farm and needed little guidance to accomplish their daily tasks.

After years of managing the family farm, the farmer decided that he would turn the business over to his four sons. Having some sense of business, he developed a corporation and divided the farm into four equal sections or organizations that would report to a single management headquarters over which he would retain control. He also set up a board of directors consisting of his four sons.

With the corporation in place, the four sons began managing their smaller farms. *Simple* awoke the first day after his father had established the corporation and began to wander his portion of the farm. He covered his entire area. The workers were there and continued to perform their daily tasks. Since it was early spring, the work consisted mostly of preparations for the spring planting. When one of the workers asked where to store the seeds that had been picked up for the upcoming planting, *Simple* gave direction. He knew how the farm operated and could easily manage the vast operation in the way his father had done. After all, he reasoned, it was only one quarter as large.

Dreamer also took a tour of his portion of the farm. He looked for ways to improve the operation. He thought, "Isn't there a way to do things differently and make more money? Isn't there something else we might do with the land that would be better than farming?" Given that the spring planting season was close at hand, there was little that he could do, at least for this season. But he had big plans for the land and would be ready to make big changes next year.

On the third parcel of land, *Jumpy* was quick to make changes. First, he reorganized the layout of the fields. He reasoned that he could use the larger field for the crops that brought in the most money. He also decided to lay off some of the workers, deciding that it cost too much to keep the staff employed throughout the year. Another major decision was to add new crops that were sure to bring in more money. All of these decisions were made rapidly and without talking to the workers first. When he announced his plans there was an immediate backlash. Several raised questions about the growing of these new crops in the region and how the crops would be planted as efficiently or even at all with unskilled labor.

Jumpy would not hear of their concerns and refused to consider their admonitions.

Wally seemed to be more pensive than his brothers. He had been walking the fields for years, so there was little use in retracing his steps. He knew the farm well. Therefore, his first step in his new position was to think about a direction for the farm. He thought about what he hoped to accomplish. Was the farm running at full capacity? Were there ways to increase the productivity of the operation? *Wally* also thought that it would be a good idea to meet with his employees, especially the managers, in order to get their input. After a very productive meeting, *Wally* was full of energy. He jotted down some ideas based on his experiences and the discussion he had just had with his employees. The ideas seemed to flow easily. There would be goals and objectives, implemented in a phased approach. To make so many changes all at once would be risky; developing the plans to make changes over time seemed prudent. For the next planting season, there would only be modest, procedural changes intended to streamline operations rather than cause wholesale change. He was very excited as he realized that he had developed a plan for his portion of the farm.

The end of the first season was very telling as the character of the four sons was revealed on the four farms. *Simple*'s farm continued in much the same manner as when the four farms were one. Crop yields were consistent and predictable. The workers continued to do their jobs and *Simple* continued to live life day to day. On *Dreamer*'s parcel, things were also much as they had been when his father ran the farm. He was anxiously waiting for the end of the harvesting season, so that he could make the major changes to the land usage that he desired.

On his parcel of the farm, *Jumpy* was in real trouble. All of the changes that he had made turned out to be problematic. The rotation of the crops to other fields in an effort to make more money did not turn out as expected. The field that the high-value crop needed to be in was fallow, and thus the yield was considerably less than *Jumpy* had hoped. The field that the lower-valued crop had been rotated into did not support the new crop because it received too much direct sunlight. Firing the workers had been a mistake; there were no longer enough skilled supervisors during the harvest season. As a result, much of the crop was lost in the field.

Sure and steady *Wally*'s portion of the farm did as one might have expected. He had only made small procedural changes based on his experience and the recommendations of the workers. *Wally* had even taken the time to tell each of his workers what the vision for the organization was and his or her role in its accomplishment. The result was a slight increase in productivity. He felt good, as his farm had taken the first steps toward reaching the productivity goals he had established for the business. There was the added benefit of his workers seeing that the farm was operating efficiently and moving toward a common purpose.

At the first board of directors meeting chaired by their father, each son reviewed his progress of the first year and discussed plans for the next season. *Wally* went first and discussed the positive increases in productivity for the year. He also provided the highlights of his program for meeting a series of goals and objectives that had been established for the next several years. Since it was clear that during the first season, *Jumpy* had had major difficulties, he thought about being more methodical and decided "on the spot" to develop a program that would allow him to reach some stated goals. Over the course of the next few minutes, *Jumpy* discussed his vision for the farm. Of course, there was little to back up his assertions or the direction he was proposing, but he felt that a program could be developed based on the vision he quickly drafted in front of the group. *Dreamer* and *Simple* said little during the course of the meeting other than to review the first season's progress. *Dreamer* sat quietly thinking of the major changes he would make to the farm during the winter, but said little about the plans. *Simple*, on the other hand, thought about nothing in particular with regard to the next season as he planned to continue the status quo.

Over the course of the winter, the differences in the four farms became even more noticeable. *Dreamer*'s long-term vision was to increase productivity by branching out into other endeavors. He had been very impressed with a bed-and-breakfast establishment that he had seen. He was also very interested in developing the land for game fishing. Of course, he knew that it would be necessary to continue to farm the land to bring in money while these other endeavors were established, so he set out to combine the three businesses into a single enterprise. He turned his old barn into a bed-and-breakfast while he dammed up the creek that ran through his property. Predictably, damming the creek took valuable land away from the farming operation. Perhaps not as predictable, at least to *Dreamer*, was that making the transition to other fields such as the game fishing and hotel business would be so difficult and require so much knowledge. Asking farm workers to move into these other businesses where they had little or no expertise turned out to be an unexpected problem. Since he no longer had a barn, his farm equipment was now exposed to the elements, creating maintenance problems, which further hindered his farming operation.

Jumpy had listened to and watched his brother, *Wally*, and had been impressed with his vision for the farm. In the hastily conceived vision *Jumpy* had presented at the board of directors meeting, he had a concept for incorporating more modern farming techniques and adding a greater variety of crops to the planting. He reasoned that having more crops would diversify the farm and provide risk protection against a bad growing season for a particular crop or a market downturn for a specific commodity. It all seemed reasonable and his father and brothers had seemed excited about and even supportive of the idea. As the vision implementation began, *Jumpy* and his workers began planting the diversified crops. Almost immediately, the bad news of a greatly reduced price for one of the new crops was reported. Shortly thereafter, there was another troubling report of severe weather that would affect another of the new crops that they had planted. By the time *Jumpy* decided to take action, they were midway through the season. Instead of staying the course, *Jumpy* decided to dig up the planting from the spring and go back to the old crops. The result once again was predictable as none of the crops, either those that were dug up in mid-season or those planted in mid-season, reached maturity. The losses were staggering and not at all well received at the board of directors meeting.

Wally continued to implement his vision. In addition to planting new, more lucrative crops, *Wally* had a plan to raise livestock. He reasoned that he would start small and continue to grow the business. That season, *Wally* began to raise cattle. The reports all indicated that there was good money to be made with little risk. Unlike with his brother *Jumpy*, when the announcement of the troubling weather reports hit, *Wally* met with his supervisors to receive their recommendations and then decided to stay the course. His farm weathered the storm quite nicely and even made some money on the crops, although it did not reach the potential that he had hoped before the planting. Despite that, *Wally* and his team learned valuable lessons about the new crops, which would be of use in the future planting seasons. Throughout the process, he knew that he would need to be patient as the business continued to grow and move the farm closer toward the vision he had outlined.

This pattern continued over the course of the years. *Simple* continued to farm the land in much the same way as his father did for years before him. His existence was as his character, from day to day. *Dreamer* and *Jumpy* continued to chase one get rich scheme after another, but had little to show for it. Both had a vision for their portion of the farm, but each allowed their character flaws to hinder the progress toward a stated vision and the accompanying goals and objectives that define that vision. *Wally* not only set realistic goals and objectives, but he measured them against the metrics that he had established and continued to grow his farm.

The Farmer's Family in the Real World

History contains many examples of the impact a *vision* can have. It is not limited to only certain fields or disciplines. From foreign affairs to the building of our nation to our national goals and objectives, vision has been a key ingredient to our success. Four historical examples are provided for consideration.

Constitutional Convention of 1787

The American colonies declared their independence from England with the signing of the Declaration of Independence in 1776. This document signified both a beginning and an end for the young nation. It was an end in the sense that governance by the British was ended, yet a beginning because it signified the birth of our nation. The Declaration of Independence was based on the premise of equality and justice for all. It recognized certain unalienable rights, including "life, liberty, and the pursuit of happiness."

From 1776 to 1787, the legal basis for cooperation between the states was established in the Articles of Confederation. This document allowed each state to remain sovereign, but levied upon the states and their citizens certain rights and responsibilities.

In 1787, fifty-five men met in Philadelphia to create a document that has become the cornerstone of our society and our democracy, the Constitution of the United States of America. This single document provides a vision for our nation consisting of seven basic articles and a preamble:

> We the people of the United States, in order to form a more perfect Union, establish Justice, insure domestic Tranquility, provide for the common defense, promote the general welfare, and secure the blessings of liberty to ourselves and our posterity, do ordain and establish the Constitution of the United States of America.

It has been and remains a touchstone document for our nation. With the ability to be amended, it continues to live and breathe just as the Founding Fathers intended. Despite all the changes, the original vision for our nation remains intact. Perhaps equally important in our discussion of vision is that the Declaration of Independence, the Articles of Confederation, and the Constitution all remain true to the original settlers who traveled to the United States to find religious and economic freedom in a new land.

Gen. Dwight D. Eisenhower

> You will enter the continent of Europe and, in conjunction with the United Nations, undertake operations aimed at the heart of Germany and the destruction of her armed forces.
>
> —Combined Chiefs' directive to Eisenhower[2]

The invasion of Europe in World War II to defeat Germany was undertaken based on a very simple and straightforward statement of purpose that was provided to General Eisenhower from the Combined Chiefs of Staff. The clear guidance was translated into an equally terse mission statement Eisenhower drafted for his invasion forces.

As the soldiers, sailors, and airmen of the Allied Expeditionary Force (AEF) embarked upon the invasion of the European continent, a communiqué from Eisenhower guided their efforts:

> You are about to embark upon a Great Crusade, towards which you have striven for many months. The eyes of the World are upon you. The hopes and prayers of liberty-loving everywhere march with you. . . . Your task will not be an easy one. Your enemy is well trained, well equipped and battle-hardened. . . . I have full confidence in your courage, devotion to duty and skill in battle. We will accept nothing less than full victory.

With these words, Eisenhower launched a force of over a million fighting men, in a campaign that would ultimately spell the defeat of the German army and surrender of Germany in 1945.

Eisenhower's personal commitment can be seen clearly in a statement made to General Bradley's officers at the height of the planning for Operation Overlord, the amphibious assault into northern France. He stated,

> This operation is not being planned with any alternatives. It is being planned as a victory, and that's the way it's going to be. We're going down there, and we're throwing everything we have into it, and we're going to make it a success.

Eisenhower's words and actions clearly provide a sense of focus, commitment, and energy that undoubtedly impacted favorably on the invasion force to accomplish the stated goal.

President John F. Kennedy

During a speech at Rice University in Houston, Texas, on September 12, 1962, President Kennedy announced a presidential initiative to go to the moon by the end of the decade. It is arguably not the most significant contribution of the Kennedy administration, but it is a clear indication of how a focused vision invested in both personally and professionally can lead to great accomplishments of a magnitude considered impossible by some. Kennedy stated in his address,

> We choose to go to the moon. We choose to go to the moon in this decade and do the other things, not because they are easy, but because they are hard, because that goal will serve to organize and measure the best of our energies and skills, because that challenge is one that we are willing to accept, one we are unwilling to postpone, and one which we intend to win, and the others, too. It is for these reasons that I regard the decision last year to shift our efforts in space from low to high gear as among the most important decisions that will be made during my incumbency in the office of the Presidency.

This initiative in the context of world events of the time did take on added significance as the United States had fallen behind the Soviet Union in the space race. Kennedy's statement of purpose was therefore as much intended to energize our scientists as well as confront the Soviets in the Cold War on another front.

The vision came to fruition in the summer of 1969 with those words uttered by astronaut Neil Armstrong, "One small step for man, one giant leap for mankind." Kennedy's vision for putting a man on the moon by the end of the decade had been reached some six years after his death.

President Ronald Reagan

When President Reagan was inaugurated as the fortieth president of the United States, national prestige, at least with respect to our role in foreign affairs, seemed to be at a low point. The nation watched as fifty-three Americans were held hostage by a third world power for 444 days, the Soviet Union's aggression seemed to be unstoppable, and U.S. military forces were at a low point in terms of capabilities and prestige.

Almost immediately after his inauguration in 1981, President Reagan set a course that reversed the trends of the post-Vietnam era. The rebuilding of the military began with significant increases in American military capabilities and spending.

Simultaneously, he began a campaign to undermine the policies of the Soviet Union. He denounced the policy of détente and exposed it as a "one-way street that the Soviet Union has used to pursue their own aims." He also began an aggressive campaign to meet the Soviets at their doorstep. He deployed Intermediate Nuclear Forces (INF) and at the same time increased the conventional capabilities of our forces as well as those of our NATO partners.

His 1983 announcement of the Strategic Defense Initiative (SDI), which he viewed as a defensive measure to protect the U.S. homeland from strategic nuclear attack, was another key measure designed to protect America and trump Soviet power.

President Reagan's vision for America as a superpower and the rebuilding of our foreign policy and military apparatus was demonstrated years after he left office in the Persian Gulf War in which a U.S.-led coalition ejected an Iraqi force from Kuwait in a 100-hour ground war. Reagan's ability to communicate his vision for America was nothing less than profound.

So What Does All This Mean?

The assertion was made previously that an effective vision must have a focus or singleness of purpose combined with energy and consistency in execution. The point should also be made that in this business of vision, two out of three is not good enough. That is, (1) focus and consistency without energy, (2) focus and energy without consistency, and (3) energy and consistency without focus are equally troubling combinations that have the propensity to adversely impact individuals or organizations.

The story of the farmer and his sons is an illustration of how important a clearly defined, energetic, and consistent vision is for an individual or organization. In the case of *Simple*, there really is no vision. He and his organization run his portion of the farm the way it has always been done, almost as if by memory. If things happen, *Simple* may react, but there is really no forward thinking or attempt to influence outcomes. *Simple* may believe that he is taking his organization in the right direction, but because of the lack of a stated or even implied vision, he and the organization will never know if a destination is reached. As the adage goes, "If you don't know where you are going, any path will get you there," and *Simple* follows it to the letter.

Dreamer demonstrates that to be useful and effective, a vision must be focused and consistent to include being grounded in reality. Clearly, there is energy in his ideas and the fact that he has a vision is good, but because the direction is so far out of bounds, it is not healthy for the organization. It goes without saying that the vision he has established is not achievable.

Jumpy moves from idea to idea so rapidly that one might say that the life span of a vision in this organization is measured in hours and days rather than in months and years. Without a consistency in action, the energy becomes unfocused and diffused. The end result is that nothing is accomplished, and there is great turbulence within the organization. Frustration in an organization such as this is both predictable and unavoidable.

Wally has struck the right balance. He is focused, has a goal, and displays great energy and consistency. He is methodical and relies on subordinates for ideas as well as buy-in for the vision for his organization. He not only develops plans for improving his organization, but also conducts periodic assessments to reorient his plan, if necessary.

Is it possible to gain a greater understanding of the role that vision plays in any organization and any set of principles that govern this quest for a vision and its implementation?

Figure 3.
Vision of the Farmer's Sons

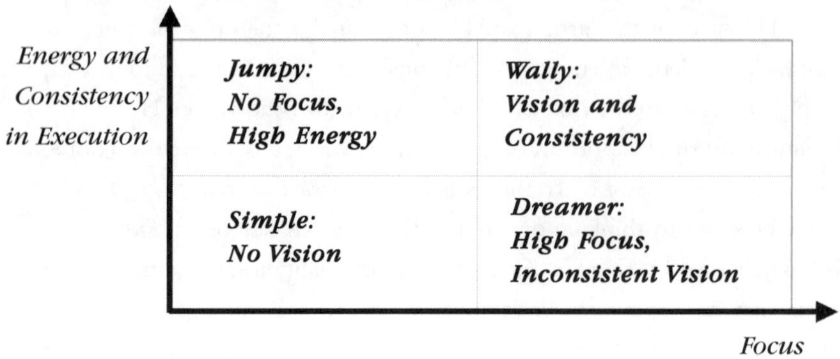

The Rules

The importance of vision has been discussed, but are there any rules? I would say yes; however, I would also caution that they are not immutable. That is, failure to follow any or all of the rules does not necessarily result in failure. Put another way, the absence of vision does not ensure failure any more than the perfect vision ensures success.

1. Have a vision. The most important thing any individual or organization can do to ensure success is to have a vision or plan. A statement of purpose that provides focus will stimulate the growth of an organization. In drafting such a statement, it is important that the vision be broad and enduring and focus on the strategic, not the tactical. But even that is not enough; the vision must have structure. This is where the vision must have accompanying goals, objectives, policies, and procedures designed to move forward toward the endstate. They chart a course for implementation that is equally important to the development of an overarching vision statement. These structural components provide measurable waypoints for the vision while the policies and procedures help to establish the framework under which the organization will operate as it moves to accomplish its vision. It is simply not enough to hope for success, but rather success must be planned, and in some detail.

2. Be consistent. The importance of consistency cannot be overstated. A leader may have a great vision statement for an organization, but if it changes frequently, then it may never be reached. Patience counts in developing and achieving a vision. An 80 percent vision executed by 100 percent of the organization's personnel is better than a 100 percent vision executed by only 80 percent. This is not to say that once a vision is announced there should be no changes, but rather that any changes should be made only sparingly and in response to results such as failing to achieve interim goals and objectives. If a new vision is published every two weeks or even quarterly, then it will lose relevance. In developing a vision statement, determine what the essence of an organization is and work to develop a plan for achieving this vision. If an organization sells real estate, but the organizational vision calls for building a jet fighter aircraft, then the vision is inconsistent with the organization and must be revised or discarded to have relevance to the organization. It takes a strong leader to see beyond the tyranny of the urgent and stay focused on the organization's vision. At the same time, the leader must be skilled enough to discern the difference between tactical, operational, and strategic events that occur in the short term.

3. Don't keep the vision a secret. Effective visions must be widely disseminated. If members of the organizations do not know or understand the vision, then they cannot possibly work to achieve it. Not disseminating the vision is like a tug-of-war where one team is pulling its section of the rope in different ways. Additionally, it is essential that leaders get "buy-in" to ensure the success of the vision. A vision with the support and even input of the subordinates within an organization will be strong and vibrant. A vision developed by a single source within an organization is harder to sell and maintain. It can still be effective, but it is harder to gain and maintain momentum, at least initially.

4. Reach is important. For a vision to be significant, it must have reach. Some may think of this as a stretch goal. Whatever one calls it, reach will cause individuals and the organization to strive for something important, and failure to accomplish something important trivializes the effort. Accomplishment of a statement of purpose in the first week after it is announced will likely not be seen as a significant event. Likewise a vision statement that is unreachable will be looked upon skeptically. It is therefore important to identify a vision with enough reach to be relevant, but not so much as to be seen to be impossible. Balance is a key ingredient in this regard. Of course, it is possible that a vision may never be fully achieved, but still be considered effective and relevant. Failure to fully achieve a vision could be related to changes in the situation or circumstances that are beyond the control of an organization. The real measure of success is the overall movement of an organization to a more favorable or advantageous position rather than a strict "Go/No Go" criteria.

5. Make the vision statement measurable. The goals, objectives, policies, and procedures that are inherent in a vision statement must be measurable. It is important for the organization to be able to measure success or determine if the path it is on will lead to accomplishment of the stated vision. The morale of the organization will actually improve as key milestones of the vision are achieved. Success will be contagious and the feeling of excellence and accomplishment will become a self-fulfilling prophecy. The statement "success breeds success" will be alive in the organization. Further, if the path the organization is on is judged to not lead to accomplishment of the stated vision, then it is possible to make a mid-course correction.

6. Energy matters. The statement of a vision is an important first step in the development of purpose and lifecycle of an organization. An equally important component of the vision process is to provide energy to move the vision forward. It is not enough to have made the statement of vision. One must invest, both personally and professionally. Once the organization has bought into the vision, directed, highly focused energy must give it the momentum necessary to carry through until completion. Any wavering by the leaders in an organization is cause for great concern, and will undoubtedly be perceived by the organization. There will be times in working toward a vision that some will waver and perhaps recommend compromising. This is not the time for the faint of heart, for leaders will be judged on how they respond when the odds look long and the support is waning.

7. Talk about the vision frequently. A direct relationship exists between the concept of the leader applying energy toward the vision and talking about the vision. Leaders at all levels within the organization must be seen to embrace the corporate vision—one way to do this is to discuss it frequently. The organization will be watching to see if a vision is being promoted or whether management is simply going through the motions. This frequent bantering about the vision will likely have a great impact on whether the vision becomes alive for an organization. For example, in major policy discussions such as a board meeting or within the corporate literature, a reference to the vision is imperative. Each time the vision or one of its components is mentioned, the vision picks up more momentum. Work it into policy speeches, into ceremonies, anywhere possible. The best vision without advertising is a little like having the greatest electronic device without electricity; both are going nowhere.

8. Intellectual action leads physical action. For years, many of us have heard the more common form of this phrase: "Think before you act." It is a key to success in working toward a vision. The physical act will be vitally important when is comes to the execution; however, before there is any movement toward accomplishing the vision, there must be a thought process that focuses on the task or tasks at hand. What is the organization trying to accomplish? In what time frames? With what material? This intellectual act must precede the physical act for success to be assured.

Developing and Maintaining a Vision

An army Field Manual from 1987 states, "To make their vision reality, senior leaders develop a game plan; establish standard rules priorities and objectives; allow time to reflect; and consider the influence of their personnel factors." The very act of developing a vision will itself be productive. An examination of the current state of affairs combined with reflection on desired endstate will be healthy for the organization. Combining this analysis with key leader discussions within an organization to gather ideas, establish a dialogue, and begin to get a buy-in will undoubtedly stimulate the organization to achieve new heights.

In thinking about developing an organizational vision, several discrete steps will be essential. They are as follows:

- Statement of organizational purpose. What are the goals of the organization? This provides the long-term focus for development of a vision.
- Listing of desired outcomes (implied and essential tasks). In strategic terms, this amounts to the ends or objectives of the strategy. Below the organizational vision are the missions that must be accomplished.
- Developing a strategic plan. The planning is concerned with the development of the ways and means of the strategy for the organization. How will the ways and means be combined to achieve the stated ends?
- Defining success. What are the measures of effectiveness? How will the organization know that it has succeeded? This may seem like an innocuous question, but it is critical to defining the endstate and knowing when it has been achieved.
- Continual assessment of vision. In any vision, there must be a continuous process of measuring the expenditure of ways and means, the movement toward the objectives and the risk of the strategy over

time. When found to be "out of alignment," changes must be made to the original strategy. Furthermore, the strategic leader must build into any vision the flexibility to respond to changes in the environment.

Vision and communication are preeminent for the Information Age leader. The pyramidal structure of the argument that has been constructed was deliberate to signify the essential role that vision and communication fulfill in this new era.

In the subsequent sections, analysis and judgment, perspective, and the three Is—imagination, innovation, and initiative—will be discussed as they too serve as important tools for the twenty-first-century Information Age leader.

Analysis and Judgment

The first of the three supports for vision and communication are analysis and judgment. How can leaders maintain agility and flexibility and be able to handle uncertainty if they always need to conduct analysis and develop carefully considered judgments?

The key is to have done the analyses in advance of operations to allow for freedom of maneuver at the point of execution. The strategic leader must understand the environment and the situation with great precision as a precursor for making decisions, and certainly prior to entering into operations or committing resources as part of the national security strategy. This includes understanding and accounting for the cultural nuances of each situation that must figure in prominently as a central component of the planning and execution process. As an example, cultural differences exist between Muslims in Bosnia-Herzegovina, Iraq, and Indonesia. Therefore, attempting to put a single ideological framework on these disparate peoples and execute a policy based on this evaluation is starting from a point of significant disadvantage.

Consider another example from the recent case of operations, in particular, writing a constitution for Iraq. Given the history of Iraq—including the formation of national borders around the country in the 1920s, occupation by the British for twelve years, and independence in 1932—and the internal ethnic and religious composition of the country, it should come as no surprise that the various factions will be challenged to develop a strong federal democratic constitution. In fact, the idea of a united Iraq, made less possible by the harsh treatment of the Kurds in the north and Shiite Muslims in the south, by Saddam Hussein and the predominantly Sunni Baathists in the central part of Iraq seems unlikely at best and impossible at worst.

The Information Age leader must learn to deal with the complex, but here it gets confusing. The leader must not only be able to deconstruct complex issues into their component parts but also learn to recompose or reconstruct systems to gain a better understanding of how they work. Let me put it in practical terms. If the tank commander has the best crew with the greatest technical proficiency, but does not understand the scheme of maneuver, then the technical skills will be of limited utility. In contrast, the tank platoon with a great understanding of the scheme of maneuver but little technical ability to engage targets will probably not contribute well to the success of the operation. In the first case, shortfalls in understanding the context are the issue, while in the second, there are technical issues associated with the crew. In neither case will the performance be optimal.

Taken to a higher level, the operation resulting in maximum casualties for non-coalition personnel may be appropriate in a hostile environment where enemy combatants are operating, but this same strategy during stability and reconstruction operations resulting in heavy non-combatant casualties is very likely to have an adverse effect.

In dealing with complex situations and systems, leaders must resist the urge to directly apply a template to a situation just because it worked elsewhere. During early stages of operations in Afghanistan in October 2001, paramilitary forces from the CIA established contact with forces from the Northern Alliances. These forces, indigenous to Afghanistan, were already doing battle with Taliban elements based on historic rivalries. When U.S. military forces were inserted shortly thereafter, they carried capabilities for forward air controlling and coordinating the efforts of the elements of the Northern Alliance. Using U.S. airpower controlled by U.S. ground forces and working with the Northern Alliance, the hastily established coalition defeated the Taliban in a matter of weeks. Many were quick to conclude that a new way of waging modern warfare had been witnessed. Given the use of advanced communications and precision weapons, the benefits of Information Age technologies were evident, but can one really conclude that indigenous forces could replace U.S. forces in this new manner of conflict?

Certainly these techniques worked for initial operations in Afghanistan, but could they be directly applied elsewhere? Some suggested the use of similar methods in the early stages of operations in Iraq in 2003. Unfortunately, the situations were not as similar as some would like to have believed and a more traditional approach to combat operations was required.

Complexity demands that each situation be analyzed and understood prior to developing a plan. Leaders can and should learn from previous strategies and operations, but to expect a direct translation fails to account for the subtle—and not-so-subtle—differences among societies, situations, and environments. Examining the current conflicts around the globe, none exactly correspond to the situation in Afghanistan, although some may allow for use of similar techniques for coordinating and working with indigenous forces.

Recalling the discussion of the changing geometry for Information Age leaders, another aspect of complexity emerges. If the leader is at the center of the flow of information (versus being at the top of the pyramid, as in the Industrial Age construct) with greater numbers of inputs streaming in than in the more traditional pyramidal structure, then the span of control or at least the span of contact increases greatly.

As the organization virtually expands, at least from the leader's perspective, what happens to the complexity facing the leader? Does twice the number of inputs merely double the complexity, or does complexity increase exponentially? The degree of complexity varies with each organization and situation.

By virtually expanding the organization and allowing more inputs to the leader, a corresponding increase in complexity and personal responsibility for the leader emerges. The number of hours in the day has not grown, so either efficiency through improved process flow, information technology, or other means must certainly assist in satisfying these new requirements. As with the example above, the growth is most likely not linear, meaning that complexity may increase several-fold based on adding even a few tasks. In contrast to the Industrial Age, where the pyramid structure actually tended to isolate the leader and at least limit direct access, the Information Age will allow and even facilitate the free flow of information unless security measures or screens are put on the leader's electronic inbox.

Another feature of the increasing complexity required in national security is developing leaders that have the ability to think about problems in multiple dimensions simultaneously. One can develop an outstanding strategy with well-defined *ends*, *ways*, *means*, and *risk* within the *environment* under consideration, but if this strategy cannot be understood and executed at the operational and tactical levels, then the likelihood of a successful outcome is in question. The grand strategy of the nation must translate into practical strategies in regions or countries that further translate into operations and tactics that are executable on the ground down to the lowest levels.

An example of multidimensional thinking pertains to the negotiations of the November 1995 Dayton Accords. These negotiations resulted in a peace settlement for Bosnia in which the former warring factions were separated and required to participate in various normalization activities with the desired end result a return of a multiethnic Bosnia into the global community. Amb. Richard Holbrooke was the head of the U.S. interagency delegation and Lt. Gen. Wesley Clark was the lead military representative on the team and the representative of the chairman of the Joint Chiefs of Staff, Gen. John Shalikashvili. In this role, General Clark was charged with ensuring that any agreement would be sufficient for a soldier on the ground to have the authorities necessary for force protection as well as to accomplish the overall goal of the peace operation.

To accomplish this, General Clark had to think at three levels simultaneously. Strategically, the operation had to accomplish President Clinton's stated goals: stop the fighting, alleviate the human suffering, have Bosnia remain a multiethnic state, and preserve the NATO alliance. Operationally, an agreement would need to provide the necessary authorities to the coalition forces under NATO command while giving the responsibilities for implementation to the former warring factions. Finally, at the tactical level, the individual soldier must be able to execute the operation and be able to protect and defend himself.

What has changed in this new Information Age is that these demands for complex thinking are being placed on leaders at lower and lower levels of command. The ability to engage in this three-dimensional analysis has moved down the chain of command to the point where platoon leaders and even individual soldiers must think and act strategically. It is quite telling that junior leaders' accounts of operations in Iraq invariably discuss a wide range of non-military issues. A combat platoon leader's account would be just as likely to discuss restoring electricity or interfacing with local leaders as combat operations.

In a briefing given by the 1st Cavalry Division Chief of Staff following the division's year-long operations in Iraq in 2005, I expected to be told about the combat operations of the division. Instead, the briefing centered around the delivery of basic services for the local population in and around Baghdad. As further evidence of this complexity, the division was able to correlate with great accuracy the relationship between the delivery of services and the level of violence. Where services to the population had increased, the level of violence was down, while in other areas where services remained at prewar levels, violence remained high.

Little in the division's collective experience, or for that matter the individual soldiers' educational backgrounds, had formally prepared the unit for this challenge. Admittedly, many had participated in peace operations in the Balkans, but the division had been organized for large-scale offensive operations with heavy, destructive weapons designed for overwhelming enemy defenses. Understanding that in the phase of the operation in which they would be participating, stability and reconstruction operations needed to be the primary focus while defeating insurgents was a secondary mission, the division learned how to run a city by meeting with local leaders from nearby Austin, Texas, located near Fort Hood. Leaders needed to not only be competent warfighters, but also city planners, negotiators, and administrators, made all the more complex by the foreign culture in which they were immersed.

In thinking about complexity, leaders must also learn to think more broadly about issues. What happens on the left and the right does matter. For years, I have heard people use the cautionary phrase to "stay in the box." The notion was that one should be concerned with what is directly within his or her delineated sector. The phrase has its roots in the development of control measures such as left and right limits and phase lines. But in the Information Age, well-defined sectors are far less relevant. The potential adversary certainly does not respect delineation around an area or agree to operate only in a set geographical boundary. Why should our leaders then restrict themselves in this way?

Furthermore, the ranges and capabilities of systems from weapons to electronic means allows for influencing and directly engaging normally well outside of geographic sectors. Should one artificially constrain effective engagements using boundaries? Or should one recognize that greater situational awareness provided through a wide range of sensors and inputs should allow for more reliance on individual discretion and less on pre-established boundaries?

I remember meeting with a U.S. ambassador representing the United States in a country in the Balkans and discussing an emerging situation in a neighboring country. The circumstances threatened to become more violent, grow larger, and brew over into his host-nation country. He made the comment that he was going to stay in his box until given guidance from Washington. It seemed to me at the time that at a minimum, a discussion between the two U.S. ambassadors and perhaps even an admonition to the host government through the U.S. ambassador would be in order to avert destabilization of that country as well. In the Information Age, where situations will become critical in compressed timelines and the potential for spillover even greater, staying in the box will be a reactive recipe and perhaps even a strategy for failure. As a footnote, it goes against corporate culture in many regards to think outside the box, but is precisely a new way of thinking that will be essential in the Information Age.

Particular importance is attached to gaining understanding of the situation and to being able to develop plans, execute operations, and, if necessary, change plans in mid-sequence to ensure the desired outcome.

A corollary to the discussion of vision and the need for analysis and judgment in strategic thought is as follows: ideals are important, but reality is important as well. National strategic decisions and their implementation must be grounded in a basis of fact and not simply wishful thinking. When developing policies and strategies, values and ideals have an important role to play, but reality must also carry considerable weight. While democracy in the Islamic world might be a desirable outcome as a long-term vision, we must also realize that the development of American democracy has evolved over 230 years and is unlike any other form of government in the world. One cannot expect that the overthrow of a tyrant and democratic elections in Iraq will necessarily result in a surrogate United States in that Islamic region.

An important part of analysis and judgment for the strategist or leader in the Information Age will be to successfully master the decision cycle. Several years ago, the army developed a concept for a holistic transformation in the service. Gen. Eric Shinseki, the chief of staff of the army, envisioned sweeping changes in doctrine, equipment, training, organization, personnel, and leadership that would move the army into the Information Age. At its core, the concept called for mastering the decision cycle by being able to "see first, understand first, act first, and finish decisively."

Seeing first was related to having the sensors, feeds, and communications capabilities to gather data from across the environment and provide it where it was required. Data required included not just military information on enemy order of battle and capabilities, but also climate data, geographic data, and biographies of military and civilian leaders. It also included the ability to see in real-time as events and deployments of forces were unfolding. In short, all information deemed necessary and useful for gaining a situational understanding would be collected for a complete analysis.

Based on these inputs, the leader and staff must analyze and synthesize the disparate data into a picture of the situation that would lead to a situational understanding of the battlespace. Not just factual information about an adversary is essential here, but also the likely intent of the adversary and possible courses of action. To conduct these sorts of assessments requires great skill and internalization of the adversary's capabilities, thinking, and culture. Thus, perspective is very important as well. The question is not "What would I do if I were the enemy?" but rather "What are my options?"

As this situational understanding is of great importance to understanding the Information Age and the learning process, this discussion bears additional contemplation. Even generating simple understanding will not be sufficient in the Information Age. Leaders must progress from data acquisition and gaining situational awareness to creating knowledge and finally wisdom. It is really in the final two steps, knowledge and wisdom, that the leader will internalize the situation and achieve the cognitive capability to act on the wisdom that is achieved. The concept of "The Continuum of Learning" is depicted in figure 4.[3]

Certainly, the Information Age will provide incredible enhancements in the ability to see. Sensors will allow for more effective and intrusive methods to be employed. Data and information will be available for the taking, and little will be remain outside the public domain. Thus, the Information Age will allow for greater manipulation of the inputs, raw data, and information into a more refined understanding of the strategic environment and the possibilities this environment presents.

Figure 4.
The Continuum of Learning

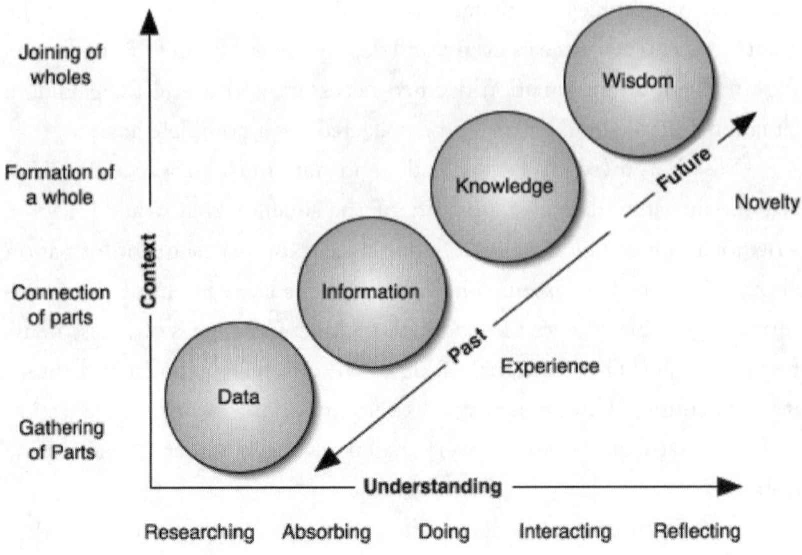

Once a true situational understanding of the adversary has been gained, the leader must have the confidence to act on the knowledge and wisdom. While the first two steps in this process—see first and understand first—involve collection and analysis, the final two steps involve the more traditional step of acting in the physical domain. The natural follow-up is to act first, which in turn leads to finishing decisively. Despite the heavy focus on the physical domain in these last two phases, information remains essential. Throughout operations, seeing and understanding continues and leads to assessing the execution of the plan, developing changes as required as a result of reaction by the opposition or the emerging situation, and determining when transition points have been reached.

Another important observation concerning the continuum of learning applies to the relationship of the continuum to the concept of employing analysis and judgment. In the data and information realms, analysis dominates. The act of compiling data from various inputs and converting to knowledge lends itself to hard analysis. Data can be stored and manipulated to arrive at information for the leader in the decision-making process. It is also largely factual. On the other hand, the conversion of information to knowledge and even more so with going from knowledge to wisdom is based largely on judgment.

Analysis also relates most closely to the science of leadership, while judgment relates more to the art. The implications here are important. Training individuals in analytical techniques is really quite straightforward. In fact, the field of operations research employs analytical techniques, albeit sometimes very complex analytical techniques, to solve difficult real-world problems and to gain insights into the functioning of complex systems. But no such field of study exists for training leaders in judgment. Perhaps the closest that the academic field comes is in the study of philosophy.

To offset this difficulty in developing judgment, strategic leaders build this data bank through training, education, and experiences. But there is also the intangible quality that largely takes us back to trait theory and the question of capacity that Jaques and Clement present in their leadership equation. Individuals have different innate capabilities; some have greater capacity for mathematics, while others are well endowed with athletic capability. In this same way, some individuals have greater capacity for judgment and reasoning that should be identified, nurtured, and used to build the bench of senior leaders in the strategy realm. More about individual capacity and identification of these individuals will be discussed later.

Even with keen personal skills for knowledge management, the volume of data and the rapidity of information flowing to the leader mandate the development of a set of decision support tools. Just as *The 9/11 Commission Report* indicates, many of the pieces of the puzzle that would have led to the discovery of the plot were available, but systemically America lacked the organization, structure, and internal coordination mechanisms between departments and agencies to turn the disparate bits of information into a threat stream that would have indicated a potential attack using civilian aircraft as weapons of mass destruction.

The twenty-first-century leader must have a different, more evolved set of tools to gain this situational understanding of the environment in which he or she operates. These tools must assist in defining an environment and classifying something (or someone) as an anomaly, aberrant behavior, or a threat. The tools must assist the leader in looking to the future rather than simply understanding the past.

On one hand, the Information Age leader must have the training, education, and experiences to rapidly gain situational understanding and act on this understanding. However, it is also necessary to temper individual experience, with factual inputs and educated assessments. Experience alone cannot be the sole source of the development of the situation. As an example, many in the summer of 2005 tried to equate the Vietnam experience to the situation in Iraq. While there are some clear parallels, there are also some dramatic differences. This shorthanded assessment normally draws an equivalence based on the insurgent nature of both conflicts, the nonmilitary requirements of "winning" the war, and the difficulties that America as a superpower is having in the prosecution of the conflict. But there are also subtle and not-so-subtle differences, such as the impact of Communist China in restraining U.S. actions in the Vietnam War, the religious aspect of the Iraq conflict, and the simple cultural differences between Vietnam and Iraq. Why should one expect that the Vietnamese and Iraqis will act in a similar fashion?

In some respects, the central point is the difference between data management and knowledge management. Consider that knowledge management includes: (1) knowledge acquisition (gathering of knowledge), (2) knowledge storage and organization (how and where data is stored), (3) knowledge distribution (a mechanism, such as an Intranet or Internet, that allows the data in the repository to be quickly disseminated throughout an organization), and (4) knowledge application (actual use of the knowledge).[4] Generally measured by its effectiveness and usefulness, knowledge management is considerably more complex than data management.

In fact, data management is a subset of knowledge management. This is an important distinction given that we spend a great deal of time, effort, and resources mining data and then managing data. Investment in intelligence capabilities for gathering data such as satellites and other technical exploitation is quite high compared with the relatively small amount spent on the higher order knowledge management. Part of this disparity is explainable given that developing knowledge is a cognitive, even highly personal endeavor that resides in the mind of the leader and the strategist.

To illustrate the difficulties with knowledge management further, Robert Sutton, a professor of organizational behavior at Stanford's University School of Engineering, says companies have wasted hundreds of millions of dollars on worthless knowledge management systems.[5] The same could be said of government management systems that have been developed to assist in sorting through the volumes of data. Below are five points made by Sutton.

- The most valuable employees often have the greatest disdain for knowledge management. Curators badger these employees to enter what they know into the system, even though few people will ever use the information.
- The managers of these systems know a lot about technology, but little about how people actually use knowledge on the job.
- Tacit knowledge is extremely difficult to capture into these systems, yet it is more critical to task performance than explicit knowledge.
- Knowledge is of little use (at least to most organizations) unless it is turned into products, services, innovations, or process improvements.
- Knowledge management systems work best when the people who

> generate the knowledge are the same people who store it, explain it to others, and coach them as they try to implement it. These systems must be managed by the people who are implementing what is known, not those who understand information technology.

Several points are worth noting with regard to Sutton's assertions. First, the ability to quantify and define knowledge management remains elusive. Leaders have a hard time objectively describing the complex decision-making process they internally employ in the formulation of actions and decisions. The collectors and managers of data and information systems have little interaction with the leaders making the decisions and gaining wisdom as a result of the inputs, so feedback to the sensors, collectors, and collators of data is rare. Just as with any system, "garbage in equals garbage out." Thus with incomplete inputs, decisions have inherently more risk. Additionally, if invalid data is entered and processed and judgment is applied, then the potential exists that "invalid" wisdom may result. One would hope that the senior leaders' judgment capabilities would alert them to something being awry, but this may not be the case 100 percent of the time.

A final interesting consideration for the discussion of Sutton's points is the relationship between the leader and the knowledge manager. The idea that knowledge management works best when the manager of the knowledge is in close proximity to the leader that implements it conjures up notions of a human hard drive walking behind the leader, ready to assist in interpreting and understanding the inputs. Actually, this concept helps to explain why the chief information officer (CIO) position has become so popular in large, complex corporations. But who is the CIO for the National Security Council, the Department of State, the Department of Defense, Department of Homeland Security, or the newly formed Director of National Intelligence? And perhaps the more relevant question is not who it is, but rather whether there is a person or organization that is responsible for the knowledge management functions in these governmental organizations, including developing knowledge and wisdom that allows freedom of action in operations and implementation of national strategy. My observation has been that even in national security or military organizations where a CIO is on the organizational wiring diagram, the duties and responsibilities fall far short of the knowledge manager envisioned in the continuum of learning or by Sutton and move into the area of information technology or an IT manager.

The Information Age dilemma deals in an area that is increasingly developing into more art than science, and more about the ability of the individual to generate and use knowledge but less about concrete measurable concepts and outcomes. Sutton claims that, in many regards, knowledge management comes down to cognitive capacity. And so the question remains of whether leaders are born or developed, according to trait theory. The important question for the most senior leaders in an organization is whether, given a certain mental capacity, Information Age leadership skills, including necessary knowledge management, can be learned and finely honed to allow for senior leadership positions. Specifically, one must determine whether transformational leaders (from the discussion of leadership theories) can develop the judgment and overall capacity to reach the highest leadership levels, or whether a lack of certain traits relegates an individual to function below the top levels.

In thinking through ways to overcome the difficulties of knowledge management and begin to develop solutions and strategies for the Information Age, several proactive approaches are worthy of consideration by the leader.

The leader must learn to organize the problem. In some respects, it goes back to having the ability to look at issues as a collection of interrelated components or as whole systems. The Information Age leader needs to be able to do both. The initial development of knowledge begins with analysis of the issue, which by definition implies an organizational construct. Leaders must also learn to manipulate the data and look at it from a variety of angles. Some may balk at the idea of leaders looking a raw data, and on a regular basis, this may not be a good use of the leader's time, but having an understanding of the inputs, data system, and information available would better prepare most leaders to develop knowledge, wisdom, and a greater appreciation for risk.

Information Age leaders in national security must also be multifaceted. A leader with a single specialty facing a complex globalized world will be disadvantaged. As part of the army's transformation process, leader characteristics were contemplated and the conclusion was drawn that leaders needed to be pentathletes rather than experts in a single area. But even the pentathlete example fails to adequately capture the agility required of the twenty-first-century Information Age leader. This emerging leader not only needs to be a pentathlete with expertise across several "sports," but also have expertise in other fields such as cultural understanding, negotiations, city planning, engineering, or information operations. Furthermore, the higher up in the national security leadership one goes, the greater the utility of having a more diverse background with multiple specialties that cut across various disciplines.

An emerging field within the area of analytical techniques that undoubtedly will gain broader use and additional relevance in the Information Age is that of link analysis and data mining. Two examples are provided; however, many more data search engines and analytical tools are available to assist in developing data, information, knowledge, and wisdom. Of note is that these tools assist more with the science of the collection and analysis process and less with the art that most closely relates to the development of wisdom.

One piece of commercially available software for conducting these analyses is called Investigative Analysis Software by i2 Limited.[6] Three tools listed include Timeline Analysis, Transaction Analysis, and Link Analysis. The purpose of each is briefly described in figure 5.

Techniques such as these continue to proliferate at an amazing rate and have broad applications for search engines or investigative work. For example, shortly after the capture of Saddam Hussein, information regarding techniques used to track his movements and contacts were described that employed methods and applications similar to the link analysis described above. By determining Hussein's inner circle and then spiraling out from there, looking at the contacts made by the people that were known contacts of Hussein's, an expanding Web was developed that allowed for tracking movements of key subordinates, planning military raids, and understanding the structure of Hussein's support while he evaded coalition forces. In the end, Hussein's capture was related to the ability to synthesize inputs from various sources into a coherent picture that allowed for executing precise military operations.

**Figure 5.
Analytical Techniques**

Timeline Analysis	Transaction Analysis	Link Analysis
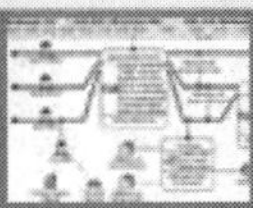	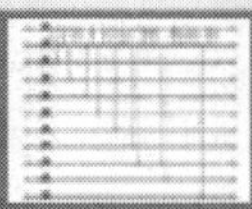	
Represents how events unfold over time by presenting them in chronological order.	Represents transactions such as bank transfers and telephones calls as links placed in chronological order.	Shows the connections or flow commodities between people, accounts, organizations, and any other element in the investigation.

Another product from Visual Analytics, Inc., provides a host of capabilities for information and knowledge management.[7] The tool provides the following capabilities:

- Integrate multiple databases from different formats and locations
- Display large volumes of data with no size limit
- Reveal direct and indirect linkages among entities
- Couple directly to existing database systems without data re-entry
- Uncover and expose interactions and relationships between all types of data
- Provide advanced analytical functions ensuring accurate pattern detection
- Perform proactive and reactive analysis supporting tactical and strategic operations
- Easily scale to support any environment
- Collaborate online with others
- Save data in a variety of formats including database, HTML, XML, image, and text files

Even products such as standard search engines like Google allow for fairly sophisticated searches of information from a variety of different sources. Given the proliferation of data mining capabilities, how does or should this change the way in which the Information Age leader operates to gain greater situational awareness and understanding?

The relevant question for the twenty-first-century leader then becomes where to spend the personal and professional time to the maximum advantage. In the military, commanders have always been taught to lead from the front and to circulate among the troops to gain a boots-on-the-ground perspective. Even Abraham Lincoln talked about the importance of visiting the front lines. But has the balance now shifted, given the amount of information one can now glean from data inputs? What is the right balance in the Information Age between data mining and analysis and circulation among the troops and visiting units for commanders in the field? The natural inclination may be for senior leaders to respond that staffs can do this sort of analytical work, but since building wisdom is a personal endeavor, some investment of the senior leader's time will be required. But how much? And who decides?

Information Age leaders must learn to conduct mental strategy simulations to examine them from various perspectives and to gain a better understanding of the sensitivities of the strategies to changes in the *ends*, *ways*, *means*, and *risk*. It is particularly important to understand the sensitivity of the strategy to the environment in which it is being applied. In these mental exercises, leaders must determine how small changes in the inputs in requirements can potentially lead to large swings in the outcome. Is it prudent to implement a strategy that is highly dependent on a single capability for success? What if this capability becomes unavailable at a critical time? Will that doom the strategy? If the answer is yes, then perhaps some mitigation is in order or the strategy should be reevaluated.

Building the right team and appropriately organizing for the mission is vitally important to the execution of any strategy. These concepts lead directly to the conclusion that a national security team must be just that—a team. This is the responsibility of the senior leader. There must be standing organizations with capabilities and leaders that have been trained and exercised for the tasks to be performed. The failed 1979 mission to rescue the American hostages held in Iran provides ample evidence of why training and rehearsals are so important in executing a strategy or a single operation. Many of the failures in the mission resulted from putting the team together at the last minute with inadequate time to train as a unit. This coupled with a changing situation that had not been anticipated, poor weather due to sandstorms, and equipment that failed en route led to a catastrophic outcome in which eight of the commandos sent in for the mission were killed when a aircraft and helicopter collided after the mission was aborted. The mission carried high risk from the start and planners and operators alike understood this, but given the lack of team training, the mission risk was accentuated.

A related concept for the leader is the requirement for continuous learning. The Information Age leader must be committed to building his or her personal library of training, education, and experiences. Think of this as building cognitive capacity. Unless one is very fortunate, the likelihood of receiving even 50 percent of the required leader skills through formal education is unlikely. It is far more probable that training, experiences, and individual efforts to learn will provide a preponderance of the knowledge and thus the cognitive capacity the leader will require for strategy development and implementation. At all points in the strategy, the leader must be gathering feeds to determine whether the strategy is working or needs to be revised. A final assessment of the outcome of a particular strategy or operation should be done to determine what worked and what should be changed for future operations. I submit that continuous learning will be more essential in the Information Age due to the vast amount of information available. Leaders that soak up information and have a larger repository of stored data, information, knowledge, and wisdom to draw from when directing the developing and executing of a strategy will have a distinct advantage.

The Information Age leader must also learn to trust his or her intuition. This is the art of leadership that served so many of America's great national security leaders so well. In this new era, with so much information available, a point in the development or execution of each strategy will come when a decision must be made and invariably the leader will feel like another piece of information is required. Unfortunately the nature of the Information Age is that one cannot afford to let pass key transition points and opportunities and thus must decide based on judgment, or what Clausewitz called *coup d'oeil.*

A best-selling book that articulates this concept well is Malcolm Gladwell's *Blink: The Power of Thinking Without Thinking*. The idea is that each person has a capability for sensing that allows him or her to innately understand situations, make assessments, and develop reactions without thinking based on first impressions, rapid cognition, and intuition. The striking example Gladwell gives in the early part of the book concerns the appraisal of a statue, purported to be an ancient work of art, that was being considered for purchase by a leading museum. Based on analysis of the statue, the conclusion was that it was several thousand years old. However, various experts who viewed the statue immediately saw aspects of the figure that caused them concern, leading to a suspicion that something was wrong with the official conclusion. It was not one particular problem with the statue that caused concern for each of them, but rather a general feeling combined with different specific anomalies. In the end, the statue was determined to be a forgery and the sale did not go through.

The front jacket of the book encapsulates the book's theme well:

> *Blink* is a book about how we think about thinking, about choices that seem to be made in an instant—in the blink of an eye—that actually aren't as simple as they seem. Why are some people brilliant decision makers, while others are consistently inept? . . . And why are the best decisions those that are impossible to explain to others?[8]

But where do the thoughts contained in *Blink* fit into the realm of strategy? Given that the book deals with human perceptions and knowledge, and that strategy is a human endeavor, it follows that elements of *Blink* dovetail into the world of the strategist. Perhaps these concepts help to explain the development of well-crafted strategies that seem to fit a situation perfectly and the leaders that are able to develop them.

Analysis and judgment will be imperatives for the Information Age leader. I certainly recognize that neither analysis nor judgment alone will be sufficient to identify successful strategies for this new era; rather, the strength comes by teaming the two concepts. Hard analysis provides a basis for making informed judgments (and sometimes these judgments will look more like intuition). While these concepts are not new, many leadership styles incorporating them are evident, and what is unique about the Information Age is the degree to which these capabilities will be increasingly demanded at lower and lower levels within the national security framework.

Perspective

The second of the three supports for vision and communication is perspective. The importance of perspective is why *environment* must be included in all future formulations of strategy. One must know how the environment will be affected by the strategy and, in turn, how the strategy will be affected by the environment. This allows for continuous refinement of the strategy to ensure that the *ends,* or the outcome, remain solidly in the center of the crosshairs.

In thinking about the development of strategy, one must realize that the direction from which the problem is approached matters. The perspective of the strategist developing and executing the strategy is considerably different than that of the nation, society, or group the strategy is targeting. In the Information Age, perspective takes on an even greater role as the ability to generate and proliferate different perspectives increases dramatically.

Just consider the multiple perspectives at work that serve to complicate execution of a coherent strategy in Iraq. Within the country there are three large ethnic groups—Sunnis, Shiites, and Kurds—each with their own perspectives. Six countries border Iraq, each with varying perspectives. Additionally, some thirty members of the coalition are participating in operations across the country; in each of the coalition countries, there are government and non-government actors, each again with different perspectives. Moving the lens over the United States, the number of "major" different perspectives is numbing as well: the president, Department of Defense, Intelligence Community, 535 members of Congress, and special interest groups, to name a few. Admittedly, there will be some overlap, but still the list is seemingly endless, and given the proliferation of information technologies to advance perspectives and opinions, the ability to develop and execute a coherent plan is greatly diminished. What this means for the leader is the requirement to recognize and understand the major varying perspectives and develop countermeasures to ensure he or she does not derail the chosen ways and means of the strategy.

Developing and employing techniques that enhance sensitivity will be imperative for the Information Age leader. You really do get a different perspective if you look up the hill to the objective, or if you are looking down the hill from the objective. To illustrate, we can use a scenario of the reader's choosing. Pick a goal that you wish to achieve. What are the *ways* and *means* that you are going to use to accomplish your objectives? Now lay out the path to get you to the objective. You have developed a plan of action based on your *ends*, *ways*, *means*, *risk*, and perspective of the *environment*. Next, put yourself on the objective, look back to your current position, and walk backward. Did the two paths align, or was the perspective such that you decided on a revised plan of execution to accomplish the stated goals? Learn to repeat the process until the two paths become one and all of the sensitivity analysis has been conducted to allow you to understand where key transition points reside and where there are potential branches and sequels for your strategy.

The simple message is that charting a course from now into the future may not be adequate. Most people are too encumbered by the here and now to allow for looking at all the possibilities for moving into the future. Keep in mind that I did not say look to the future, but rather to transport oneself into the future. Consider the example of the Joint Tactical Radio System (JTRS). Given the goal of developing a joint capable voice and data system that can operate in multiple waveforms and replaces the current families of tactical radios will yield a much different solution than looking for a system that allows for voice and data networked system for tactical operations.

The Information Age leader must also learn how to stay away from the trees when looking at the forest. This will become more difficult as the proliferation of data continues to increase rapidly. Perhaps this statement leads to some confusion, as one may ask at this point how to go from data and information to knowledge and wisdom without getting at least partway into the forest. This is the art of leadership. The leader, in particular the Information Age leader, will be bombarded with data and information. The key will be to discern the important information from the unimportant information. Notice that the term "irrelevant" has not been used—even information not central to one particular strategy may be highly relevant to some future strategy and certainly contributes to the leader's overall body of knowledge and wisdom.

Consider what happens to the leader in the middle of the forest looking at the trees. The mind becomes consumed with the immediate view to the front at the expense of the broader context of what is happening to the forest. One hundred yards away, a raging fire could be consuming the forest, yet the obstructed view does not allow the fire to be seen. Only by zooming out and gaining a modicum of perspective can the true situation be assessed.

Another drawback to being in the forest besides the limited view is the absorption capability of the human mind. If the focus of one's attention is from inside the forest, the view will include the tree to the front and the scene immediately around the area—the leaves on the ground, the sap rolling down the individual tree, the trees to the left and right. This is where the viewer's attention will be. Since the human mind can only absorb finite amounts of information in a period of time and the human processor has a certain capacity as well, a forest-level view (even if one could have a split-screen view) would still detract from developing the broader perspective.

Revisiting another critical topic, it is imperative that Information Age leaders be able to think on several levels simultaneously. Earlier we referred to this as being able to play a three-dimensional chess game—the ability of the leader to simulate in his or her mind the various levels on which a strategy will be implemented. Consider again the Bosnia peace negotiations. Holbrooke and Clark needed to ensure that all levels of interaction (or command) could adequately implement the negotiated settlement. That meant that at the international level, nations would agree and support the plan; at the national political level, the U.S. Congress would ratify the treaty; at the strategic, operational, and tactical levels of conflict, military forces and interagency representatives could implement the full measure of the agreement; and finally that the former warring factions agreed and had a reasonable expectation that the outcome would succeed. There were certainly a number of levels on which the negotiating team needed to function to assure a viable outcome.

In this multilevel analysis, leaders must be able to understand how each of the parties will perceive and act on the strategies under consideration. It is imperative to be able to understand the issues from each vantage point.

A final necessity under the heading of perspective is being able to argue both sides of an issue. By this, I mean that in articulating one position, a useful exercise is to make the opposite case. I submit that it will assist in better understanding one's own position and most likely provide significant insights into why actors respond in certain ways.

All too often in discussions of strategy, strategists develop a position and have very cogent arguments for their recommended outcomes and strategies. In developing the rational argument for their case, a certain amount of buy-in occurs which tends to mask other ideas and positions. This phenomenon can even be worse in groups where the potential for group think is high, especially in emotionally charged discussions in which a single voice or position dominates the discussion. This tendency to fixate on a single course of action at the exclusion of all else creates a kind of myopic thinking, or group think, that is very dangerous for the development of strategies by leaders; it can result in one-sided analysis and formulations that fail to account for the environment. In such a strategy, one of the five components is inadequately addressed.

As the Information Age leader cannot hope to develop reasonable strategies without maintaining perspective, the use of a "red team," or group designed to take the position of the other actors, can be extremely important in identifying a range of possible outcomes. The term "red team" has its roots in military and intelligence work. In military training, an opposing force (OPFOR) is incorporated to add to the realism of war games and to provide a thinking adversary to train against. The Intelligence Community also uses the term to describe analysis to gain understanding and perspective of what the threat might do given a certain set of circumstances. The idea is that a red team would be given latitude to develop out-of-the-box threats and solutions.

Imagination, Innovation, and Initiative

The third of the three supports for vision and communication is imagination, innovation, and initiative. Of course, the three Is cannot exist in isolation of the vision and intent of the leader or the strategy under consideration.

These components will take on new importance in the Information Age. Creative thinking that results in imaginative and innovative solutions will be essential to maximize the potential of this new era. Many will have the wherewithal to take existing strategies and make them better and faster by applying information technologies, but the real benefits will be for those leaders able to develop new *ways* and *means* at lower risk to accomplish lofty ends within this new environment. The ability to act on these strategies, sometimes in the face of great odds will also be important, as failure to do so squanders opportunities.

There is no shortage of "sausage makers" able to take existing processes and automate them, but there will be far fewer with the insight and vision to make real change. This will separate the true innovators and creators from the processors. The real increases in efficiency and effectiveness will come from the application of the three Is and not the people turning the crank.

Imagination

Imagination is defined as "the act or power of forming a mental image of something not present to the senses or never before wholly perceived in reality; creative ability; ability to confront and deal with a problem."[9] Should leaders be dealing with things not wholly perceived in reality? Or should a firm foundation be used in the development and execution of national security strategy? The answer is both. This may sound very similar to the discussion of perspective above, most particularly the need to understand the perspective of each of the actors involved in a particular strategy. Indeed some similarities do exist.

The Information Age leader must have the ability to project his or her thoughts into the future, to imagine things that have not unfolded and possibilities that exist. At the same time, this escape from reality must arrive at strategies and thoughts that are within the range of possible outcomes that exist. To arrive at outlandish, infeasible outcomes does nothing to advance the development of a coherent vision or strategy for implementation.

The development of stealth technologies did not happen because scientists and engineers adhered to the known, but rather because they dared to think in new and creative ways. Since World War II, we have understood radar applications, but would it be possible to alter the environment through various techniques to allow for aircraft to virtually disappear from radar screens? We now know that the answer is yes. Early stealth pioneers dared to think outside the box, beyond the known.

The development of the Internet provides another example of imagination in action. Even today, most people cannot fathom the vast networks of routers, hubs, modems, switches, and Internet service providers (ISPs) connected by transmission lines. But they do exist, despite the fact that most of us only know that our computer at home connects to a cable or telephone line in the wall and we have global connectivity. In the 1980s, pioneers dared to imagine a time when electronic information would flow almost anywhere, and vast data networks would be built to support the massive flow of data.

The battle plan for the initial stages of operations in Afghanistan in October 2001 demonstrates equal imagination. The plan also illustrates the capacity of network-centric warfare. Who would have conceived of a plan by which an army Special Forces soldier on horseback in Afghanistan sending location data via satellite from his notebook computer to an air force B-52 bomber crew, which could drop precision-guided bombs on Taliban troops less than twenty minutes later?[10]

A mantra for imagination is "be creative." Instead of the linear ODDDA loop where the decision cycle progresses calls for observing, detecting, deciding, delivering, and assessing, a new system of polling could be developed whereby each step is conducted every five minutes and the results updated for the decision maker after each poll is taken.

Innovation

Innovation is "the introduction of something new; a new idea, method, or device."[11] The simple act of taking an Industrial Age system or process and updating it with information technologies does not result in true innovation. Many believe that putting computers in the workplace results in innovation. I would argue that simply updating the office with computers may result in more updated surroundings or even greater capacity, but unless a process is changed or positions eliminated, the office will be business as usual, albeit with people now surfing the web.

True innovation is more about the business of introducing something new. In a strategic sense, it could be a new piece of equipment or a new tactic. The introduction of the tank in World War I fits into this category, as does the introduction of blitzkrieg in World War II, which represented a new application of the operational art combining the maneuverability and speed of the tank with the firepower of artillery to overwhelm and break through enemy defense and attack rear areas.

Many hail the F-22 fighter or the Joint Strike Fighter (JSF) as an innovative aircraft. But the F-22 is really just an updated system designed to do the same task better and faster. On the other hand, the overlaying of an information network on top of the battlespace that provides digital links between the services and all elements has a more innovative quality.

Perhaps one of the most important aspects of innovation is how change or potential change is viewed within an organization. When any sort of change is announced, from a simple scheduling modification to the complete overhaul of the organization, one of a handful of reactions is likely to occur. Many will describe with great precision why the initiative will not work. Others may indifferently go back to work, confident that the initiative will die of its own weight. Still others may decide that they can wait it out and that the leader will depart or change directions before the initiative is implemented. A subset may also begin to examine how such an initiative might be implemented. But it is very likely that few will be quick to embrace change. This is the nature of organizational inertia.

Organizations and the individuals in them tend to become comfortable with routines and the familiar. An announcement of a change means going into the uncertain. And few will be excited by this. For this reason, when change is announced, the leader must be quick to communicate the change, embrace it and talk about it frequently. Any perceived hesitation will only embolden the masses.

Such was the case when General Shinseki announced the army's transformation in 1999. Naysayers initially outnumbered supporters of the plan. However, Shinseki's personal investment helped shape the plan, which then gained momentum. In 2001, Secretary of Defense Rumsfeld also propelled the plan forward. Few were immediately convinced, and, in fact, as of mid-2006, little real transformation has occurred within the department at the higher levels. Certainly the services have individual plans for transformation and are in various stages of execution of these plans. September 11 acted as an accelerant for change in the establishment of a joint four-star headquarters with responsibilities for the operations in the continental United States and military interface with and support to the new Department of Homeland Security.

If one considers implementation change in large organizations, innovation can be evolutionary or revolutionary. The likelihood is that smaller changes will elicit less organizational backwash than wholesale revolutionary change. An example of evolutionary change would be spiraling new technologies or processes into the army such as new digital communications equipment, night vision devices, or new TTPs (tactics, techniques, and procedures) for countering enemy tactics. Revolutionary change, in contrast, would be the announcement of an establishment of a Department of Homeland Security or the Director of National Intelligence, two new organizations within the U.S. government.

Two initiatives for implementing change that have gained wide acceptance in industry are Lean and Six Sigma. Lean refers to conducting value stream mapping or work flow analysis to determine what processes are not required and thus can be eliminated or can be modified to be more efficient. Anecdotal stories about implementing Lean in organizations show significant efficiencies while at the same time improving the work flow. This is done through conducting a series of passes through the process flow to eliminate any waste in the process. The intent is to eliminate any waste resulting from one of seven causes: overproduction, producing defects, movement or transportation, inventory, overprocessing, or adding nonessential labor, waiting time, or unnecessary motion.

Six Sigma, on the other hand, refers to reducing variance and has greatest application for examining repetitive tasks. While savings generally are not as significant in Six Sigma, the major benefits are in improving quality and standardization of tasks. By examining tasks and establishing procedures, standards, and quality measures, variance is greatly reduced thus ensuring a standard level of service.

These two change management techniques are not presented by way of endorsements, but rather to use as examples of some transformational initiatives that are in used in industry as well as in some sectors involved with national security, and also to highlight implications for leaders of organizations undergoing these changes. Given these savings and improvements, the leader has a new task: to determine what to do with the personnel, space, time, and dollars that have been saved.

Consider the following examples from a briefing by Lean Investments, LLC, concerning the application of the Lean methodology.[12]

Table 3. Lean Examples

Example	Findings
Toyota	• Customer complaints down 1000 percent • Productivity up 400 percent • Space utilization down 90 percent
Naval Air Command—North Island	• $10 million in labor savings • Average turn around time reduced 74 percent • Freed up 21,196 square feet of floor space • Reduced $6.5 million in waste in process • Identified $6 million in unneeded equipment
Red River Army Depot (Truck recapitalization)	• Increased output by 220 percent • Went from 1,751 to 770 hours per vehicle for recapitalization of systems
C-130J Aircraft Maintenance	• Reduced time for fault diagnosis and servicing by 67 percent • Improved fault diagnosis by 77 percent

Imagine the reception the commander of the Naval Air Command would receive in discussing the personnel "savings" of $10 million in labor costs. That translates to lost jobs, certainly not a topic that most work forces would embrace.

As with anything new, there will invariably be those that explain in great detail why a plan cannot or will not work, but just as Lincoln did, one must find a Grant, impart the vision, and follow through on the execution. The leader must not allow the first line of resistance to be the end of the road.

In all innovation, the leader becomes the focal point. Much responsibility rests on the shoulders of the leader to explain the changes, develop excitement in the organization about the initiatives, continuously reinforce the change messages, develop measurable metrics for assessing the progress, and reward the individuals and the organization for successful innovation.

The Information Age will present great opportunities for innovation and creativity. The leader must be the change agent and the cheerleader. Note that the term "manager" was not used here. The leader will set the conditions for change, while the manager can supervise the daily business of the organization.

Initiative

Initiative is defined as the "the power or ability to begin or to follow through energetically with a plan or task; enterprise and determination; a beginning or introductory step; an opening move."[13]

A book that provides a memorable anecdote for thinking about the topic of initiative is Elbert Hubbard's *A Message to Garcia.*[14] By the author's own account, the book was written in a single hour as a record of an extraordinary act by a very junior officer given an equally extraordinary requirement on behalf of the president of the United States.

But *A Message to Garcia* describes more than just simple initiative; it portrays a maturity of thought that is essential in leaders in the fast-paced Information Age. It is about a man who dared to take a difficult and dangerous assignment without questions and disclaimers.

The story in the book goes as follows. In 1899, the United States was about to enter a war with the Spanish over the island of Cuba. The Spanish-American war would be important in U.S. history because it marked the first time that U.S. forces would be involved in operations to influence affairs of a sovereign nation. The president needed to get a message to General Garcia, a rebel leader in Cuba. He was reported to be in a remote location where no mail or telegraph could reach him. Thus the president's dilemma was how to get the message to Garcia.

Someone suggested a young lieutenant named Andrew Summers Rowan to accomplish the task. He was summoned to the president and personally given a message to hand carry to General Garcia. He took the letter and went about preparations for his trip. Four days later, Rowan landed on the shores of Cuba and began the journey to find Garcia. Three weeks later, he emerged from the jungle, having accomplished his mission.

Hubbard goes on to discuss the magnificence of the accomplishment by asking the reader to conduct a test as follows:

> You are sitting now in your office—six clerks are within call. Summon any one and make this request: "Please look in the encyclopedia and make a brief memorandum for me concerning the life of Correggio." Will the clerk quietly say, "Yes, sir," and go do the task?
>
> On your life, he will not. He will look at you out of a fishy eye and ask one or more of the following questions: Who was he? Which encyclopedia? Where is the encyclopedia? Was I hired for that? Don't you mean Bismarck? What's the matter with Charlie doing it? Is he dead? Is there any hurry? Shan't I bring you the book and let you look it up yourself? What do you want to know for?
>
> And I will lay you ten to one that after you have answered the questions, and explained how to find the information, and why you want it, the clerk will go off and get one of the other clerks to help him try to find Garcia—and then come back and tell you there is no such man. Of course I may lose my bet, but according to the Law of Average, I will not.[15]

Hubbard observed that the "the hero is the man who does his work—who carries the message to Garcia."[16] The book goes on to laud the accomplishment of Rowan in being able to get the message to Garcia. But the real point, as you can easily see is that Rowan takes the mission and on his own initiative determines how to accomplish it. There are no questions and no hesitation.

Just as Rowan became a hero of the Spanish-American War, in the

Information Age, leaders who have the situational understanding, initiative, and drive to accomplish the mission in the face of uncertainty and ambiguity will be the heroes of tomorrow. The Information Age will not permit the luxury of asking a litany of questions, but rather the knowledge, wisdom, creativity, and judgment of the leader must be allowed and encouraged to arrive at solutions to complex, even seemingly intractable problems with a minimum of guidance, direction, or elaboration.

Next Generation Information Age Leader

The leader has two vital and complementary roles that must be fulfilled simultaneously. The first, more traditional role is to lead his or her subordinates and set the conditions for the organization to accomplish the objectives that have been established. A second equally important role is the development of the next generation of leaders. The leader must always keep an eye out for candidates to succeed him or her. If no one is capable of doing so, then the leader has failed.

In this section, the changes in leadership requirements will be reexamined using the equation from the chapter 2. Additionally, the concept of developing leadership capability is considered. What can be done to assess the next generation and prepare junior leaders for increasing levels of responsibility? The concept of mentorship is also discussed as the final major topic in this section. What is the role of the mentor? How should the mentor teach and coach to impart the lessons of leadership to the next generation?

And Now Back to the Equation

As promised earlier, the leadership capacity equation from chapter 2 will be revisited to identify how it might be revised in light of the anticipated changes of the Information Age.

By way of a disclaimer, I must state once again that in no way can leadership be reduced to a simple listing of traits. In fact, leadership is much like the development of strategy in which the strategist in a specific *environment* combines *ways* and *means* to achieve *ends* while assuming *risk*. For the leader, the traits or attributes are the means that can be applied and combined in certain ways to achieve a desired outcome in specific situations.

Several concepts are important here. First, leadership is a human endeavor that remains situational. What works in one instance may fail in others. The ways in which personal qualities and traits are brought together matter greatly. If there is too much supervision, it is micromanagement; too little, it is neglect. Thus, balance remains an essential component in any leadership "calculation." The original equation was:

Current Actual Capacity (CAC) = CP + V + K/S + Wi – T, where

CP = Cognitive power (cognitive complexity, or the innate mental ability to organize information)

V = Values (interests, priorities)

K/S = Skilled use of relevant knowledge

Wi = Wisdom about people and things

T = Serious personality (temperamental) defects

It certainly seems that the elements of the equation will remain important in the Information Age. Perhaps the question is really are the ingredients in the right proportions and what is missing?

Recall the four areas that were identified as reflecting a necessary change in leadership as we transition our thinking from the Industrial Age to the Information Age. What changes to our equation would be required to more fully account for this new capacity quotient in this new environment? Remembering that the four areas are (1) vision and communication, (2) analysis and judgment, (3) perspective, and (4) the three Is—imagination, innovation, and initiative—try to consider the adaptations that would work best.

The skilled use of relevant knowledge (K/S) and the wisdom about people and things (Wi) begin to capture the essence of the change that will be required. However, components that are missing explicitly as society moves to the Information Age are imagination, innovation, and initiative that will become more critical to the development of strategies for the globalized world of the twenty-first century. Opportunities and challenges will present themselves rapidly and require creative solutions. And to complicate the issue, leaders at lower and lower levels within organizations must have these capabilities. Another important addition to this concept is the incorporation of a higher level of judgment. The term "wisdom" from the original equation implies judgment, but for the Information Age, judgment will take on an even greater significance.

Thus the update for the equation for the Information Age would modify the terms such that knowledge and wisdom would be raised to a power equal to the sum of imagination (Im), innovation (In), initiative (It), and judgment (J):

$$(K/S + Wi)^{(Im + In + It + J)}$$

This modification then accounts for the requirement for creative thinking and new concepts in the development of knowledge and wisdom. Without this modification, knowledge and skills would remain grounded in the present, lacking the reach to take advantage of this new information-dense environment. Initiative will be essential as the Information Age will present rapidly changing situations, and only those with this quality will be able to seize the moment.

Cognitive power will also require changes. The ability to incorporate perspective into one's thinking will be a decided advantage in the Information Age. Understanding all aspects of an issue can only assist in development of coherent strategies that can be implemented with a reasonable chance of success. To this end, the cognitive power (CP) component of the equation must be updated to account for the requirement for perspective (Pe) in strategic thought. This modification fits well as both the cognitive power and perspective speak to the ability of an individual to handle complexity.

Another component that must carry additional emphasis in the Information Age is the ability to organize information, or analysis (A). The vast amounts of data that will be available and must be turned into information, knowledge, and finally wisdom, require a higher level of analytical capability. Thus the term for "cognitive power" would be updated as follows:

$$CP^{(Pe + A)}$$

At this point, the original equation for "current actual capacity" has been modified to the following highly complex form:

$$CAC = CP^{(Pe + A)} + V + (K/S + Wi)^{(Im + In + It + J)} - T$$

However, we are not finished yet. The equation does not account for the most important aspects of leadership in the Information Age: vision and communication. Without these two characteristics, it is hard to imagine a twenty-first-century leader, or any leader for that matter, being successful. Throughout chapter 2, the importance of these characteristics, of having and communicating a vision, has been discussed in theory as well as in the words of the leader. In fact, at the core, these two characteristics are really the essence of twenty-first-century leadership.

The knowledge and wisdom coupled with the imagination, innovation, initiative, and judgment all go into the development of a vision or a strategic end. The cognitive power as well, modified by perspective and analytical capability, is central to the development of a coherent and feasible vision. Therefore, the original discussion of vision, when one of the definitions is related to a fortuneteller or prophet, actually has some application in our discussion of leadership, for what the leader really does is set the conditions for the future. To do this requires a certain degree of foresight, not unlike the fortuneteller or prophet.

But in this conceptual formulation, having a vision does not lead to success without the ability to communicate the vision and therefore, the original equation is further modified to the highly complex formulation:

$CAC = [CP^{(Pe + A)} + V + (K/S + Wi)^{(Im + In + It + J)} - T]^{ViC}$, where

CP = Cognitive power (cognitive complexity, or the innate mental ability to organize information)

V = Values (interests, priorities)

K/S = Skilled use of relevant knowledge

Wi = Wisdom about people and things

T = Serious personality (temperamental) defects

Pe = Perspective

A = Analytical capability

Im = Imagination

In = Innovative skills

It = Initiative

J = Judgment
ViC = Vision and communication

Note that no changes were made to the values (V) and temperamental defects (T) terms. This is no way signals that they are no longer important in the leadership formulation, but rather that they remain as they are today—critical elements for any strategic leader.

Hopefully the reader has not abandoned the quest for understanding the new leadership requirements of the Information Age given the daunting task of decomposing and interpreting this complex equation, but will be interested in further pursuit of greater understanding of how this new twenty-first-century environment will impact on the demands of the individual leader.

Thinking further about this equation, one striking aspect is that it pertains to the current actual capability—that is, the capability that the leader displays at the moment. It does not address the developmental aspects of leadership or how leaders evolve (and perhaps even devolve) over time. The subject of the next section will be to examine the more transitory nature of leadership, specifically the development of the future Information Age strategic leaders.

Before leaving this section, a useful exercise would be to examine more fully the idea of the leader skills that will gain increased importance during the Information Age. As a basis for this analysis, consider the army officer efficiency report (OER) that is assessed annually or upon the departure of the officer's immediate rater. It is both a developmental tool for the officer to assess and encourage growth as well as a way to identify those officers with potential for advancement, command, or special assignments. The OER lists a set of twenty-three leader traits broken down into four areas: attributes, skills, actions, and values.

The question then becomes, in the Information Age, will there be a change to the traits that are more relevant to the necessary skills of the twenty-first-century leader? When answering this question, try to put yourself into a situation and visualize the requirements using today's capabilities and then run the test a second time working through the anticipated changes as a result of globalization, infusion of information technologies, and knowledge management enhancements in the Information Age. What is different?

Figure 6 represents the author's assessment of likely increases on requirements for the leader in the Information Age.

The attributes describe the ways in which the officer operates. Furthermore, each individual operates in the three areas (mental, physical, emotional) simultaneously in exercising leadership. However, I believe that of the attributes, the mental, which corresponds most closely to the cognitive domain in the OSD model, will place significant and increasing demands on the Information Age leader. The physical and emotional requirements can be expected to remain just as important as they are today. Mental capacity, which can be measured (at least in theory) by the equation developed previously, will force the Information Age leader to hone his or her intellectual capacity and gain increasing ability to operate in the highly complex cognitive domain.

Unfortunately for future leaders, the demands for individual skills will rise even as more will be demanded of the Information Age leader. The strong case has been made for developing leaders with the necessary intellectual capacity to deal with multiple and changing situations. This requires conceptual thinkers, leaders who can develop the situational understanding that comes from going from data collection to wisdom.

National security leaders will also need to cultivate more highly developed skills for dealing with individuals, societies, and cultures that may be very different from our own, placing a higher demand on interpersonal skills. These skills will also be important for developing future leaders and dealing within disparate organizations and agencies within our own government such as within the interagency.

Given the increasing complexity of the world in which the strategic leader will operate, technical and tactical skills will also gain new importance. The national security leader or commander must not only be versed in the tactical formations of his or her organization or forces, but also understand how to operate in an ambiguous, changing, and complex situation where allies, coalition members, neutrals, and adversaries are ill defined. This leader must also understand the capabilities of the U.S. "forces" operating to the left and right that are likely to include civilian interagency participants.

Figure 6.
Impact of the Information Age on Army Officer Attributes

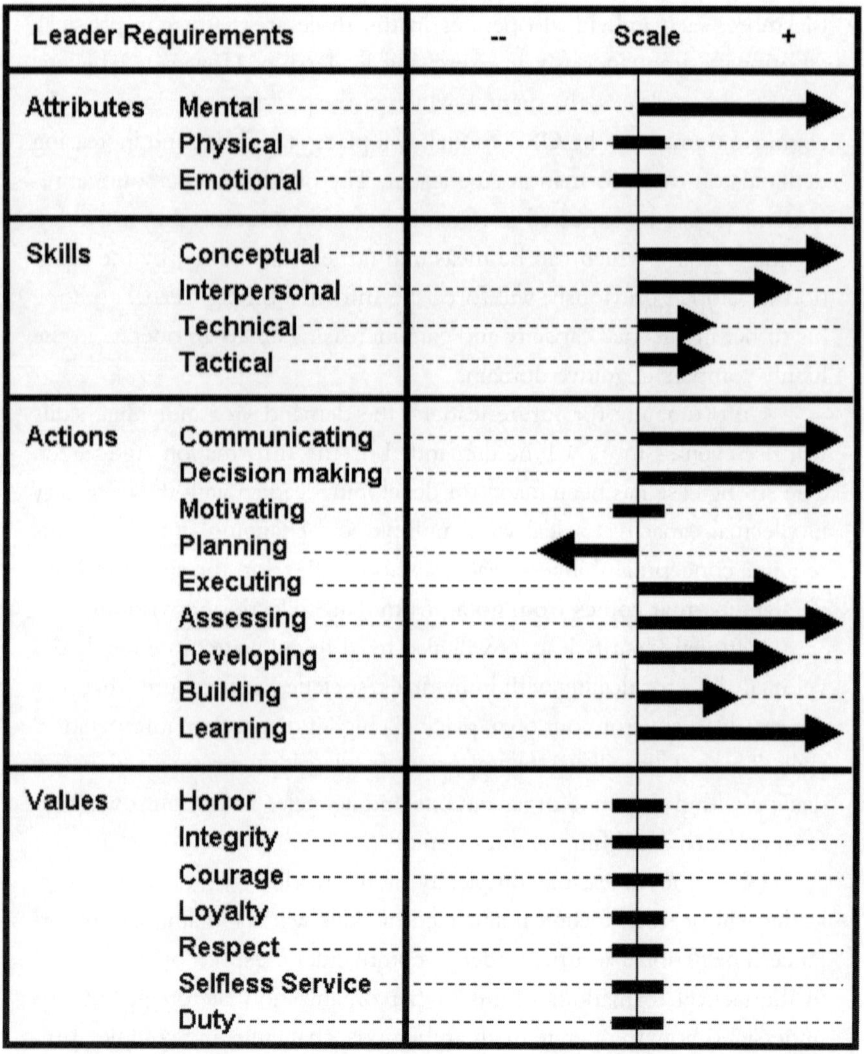

It should come as no surprise that in an era in which the time, space, and ideological relationships are altered, that "actions" required of leaders will place increased demands on the individual. In my assessment in seven of the nine categories, there will be greater demands. Only in planning, where the pendulum will swing from planning to execution and motivating, which will remain with the same approximate weight of today, will there not be an increased requirement for the leader. The skills associated with communicating and decision making, along with the execution requirements for executing and assessing, and the adaptive skills of developing, building, and learning will all gain greater importance.

Finally, in the category of values, no increase or decrease has been identified. Some may take exception to this and believe that with the greater physical separation between the leader and subordinates, values such as integrity and honor will become more important. Certainly this argument could be made and must be determined based on each situation. The author would not take offense to this categorization as it would once again demonstrate the central point that the Information Age will place greater demands on leaders.

Another note concerns the importance of the situation in which the leader is involved in determining the relative importance of these characteristics. The president's national security adviser is likely to see certain of these traits as more important while the four-star theater commander on the ground responsible for a 140,000-person force is likely to have a different perspective, which in turn will most likely cause a different valuation of some of the traits. The same would be true in comparing the brigade commander to his or her interagency counterpart, or to a platoon leader in the brigade at the tip of the spear executing low level missions.

Before leaving this topic, a worthy consideration is whether this list represents well the requirements of the Information Age leader. In the previous section, the concept of increasing the leader skill set with additional emphasis on perspective, analytical capability, imagination, innovative skills, initiative, judgment, vision, and communications was introduced. Does this set of leader requirements adequately represent the emerging requirements of the Information Age leader? I believe, unfortunately, that the answer is probably not, at least not for senior strategic leaders.

The leader requirements from the army OER were developed in the in the mid-1990s and are more representative of the Industrial Age roots than of the emerging Information Age. Over the ten years or so from the mid-1990s to the mid-2000s, the expansion of information technologies, the emergence of globalization as a very real phenomenon, and growing global interactions have combined to create a situation in the early years of the Information Age where a revision of these leader requirements is clearly in order.

For example, the original list does not include any explicit discussion of the three Is (imagination, innovation, and initiative). Neither is there an explicit requirement for developing judgment and wisdom for army leadership, or for using perspective in the decision making process. Some may be tempted to make the case that "assessing" in the original lists includes judgment and innovation, but I believe that explicit consideration of these leadership requirements is necessary for instilling the appropriate level of importance for these characteristics.

I will again make the point that each situation is different and thus leader requirements within each situation vary. The level on which the leader operates also determines the degree to which each of the listed requirements or the proposed enhancements to the list will be required. The more senior strategic leaders will need to place more emphasis on the higher order skills of the Information Age while the more junior leaders will likely have more requirements for skills associated with executing assigned missions. Despite this potentially sliding scale for the application of leader requirements, it is important to consider that the junior leaders of today are the senior leaders of tomorrow, and thus, adequate attention must be given the development of the future generations of strategic leaders. Therefore, the responsibility of the senior strategic leader is to instill in his or her subordinates the requisite skills and developmental experiences. It is also the responsibility of the senior leaders of today to identify these emerging strategic leaders.

Identifying and Developing the Next Generation Information Age Leader

As with any process, it takes time and effort to grow leaders. Take the example of the uniformed leader. The progression from lieutenant to general takes over thirty years, not including up to four additional years of pre-commissioning training and education. The same is true for the corps of professional ambassadors. Foreign service officers also have a twenty-five- to thirty-year developmental period before appointment as an ambassador. And in both of these fields there is a formal system of training, education, and experiences that contribute to the development of these officers. Other professions including the legal and medical fields have systems that allow for development and progression. Certainly one does not go from law school to the Supreme Court overnight.

Given the length of time and importance of grooming the next generation of national security leader, some time should go into selecting the right people for close monitoring, careful development, and advancement into strategic leadership positions.

Whether one ascribes to the trait, situational, or transformational theories of leadership, a reasonable assumption is that people have certain capacities that are based on a variety of factors including personality, education, experiences, training, and even individual preferences. In a briefing in 1991 to Gen. Maxwell Thurman, then the vice chief of staff of the army, the concept of capacity was portrayed in a series of curves where the y axis was the capacity and the x axis was the time in years of an individual.[17] The graph demonstrated that over time, an individual's capacity increased as a result of increasing maturity. The theory allows that individuals begin at different points in the curve and thus have more or less initial capacity (see figure 7).

The capacity over time also changes as a result of stimuli. In the figure, the position at age twenty-five years would place the individual on a trajectory that would have a capacity of A75 at age seventy-five years. However, with a concerted effort to train, educate, provide developmental experiences, and mentor, perhaps the individual's capacity can be raised to the higher position delineated by $A_{New}{}^{75}$ by following the trajectory represented by the dotted line in the figure.

The point is that capacity is not static. Consider the case of an officer in the military. Training provides the individual, in this case an army officer, with additional skills and experiences that build the reservoir on

Figure 7.
Individual Capacity Development

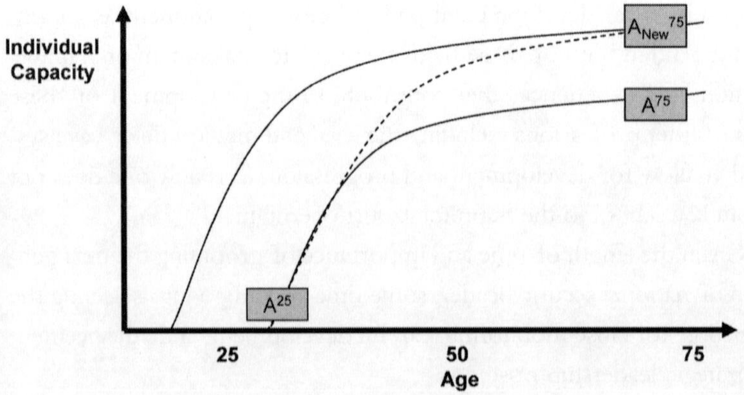

1. People start at different levels.
2. People mature at different levels.
3. Training, education, experiences, and mentorship can change the trajectory of an individual's capacity.

which the individual can draw. Early in their careers, army officers attend basic branch qualification schools to learn the skills required of a tanker, a logistician, or a signaler, for example. Then at various points in an officer's career, he or she returns to the military schoolhouse to learn additional skills. An average officer will spend 20 to 25 percent of the first twenty years of a career in military schools. Select individuals go to civilian schools to pursue advanced degrees as well.

All this formal training and education prepares the individual for greater levels of responsibility and enhances capacity. Training and experiences are also acquired in less formal settings either in unit training or through developmental assignments. When a leader takes an army unit to the National Training Center at Fort Irwin, California, or an air force unit to Red Flag at Nellis Air Force Base, Nevada, the unit develops a set of experiences that is coming as close to actual combat as possible in a training environment. Assignment to the Pentagon provides the officer with a corporate view of the military allowing one to gain a broader perspective.

In each of the services, there are required steps in a career path. In the air force, after pilot training, individual pilots seek to become qualified in a specific aircraft, become a pilot in command, a flight lead, squadron commander, and then wing commander. These positions provide key experiences and training that contribute to the individual's capacity. This same concept holds true for the foreign service where career development calls for a long series of positions prior to being appointed an ambassador.

Individuals who display either an advanced initial capacity or rapid matriculation potential must be identified and provided with more and greater opportunities for developing their individual reservoirs. This includes matriculation into the right developmental assignments to ensure that their full potential is realized. The White House Fellowship program seeks as a stated purpose to provide opportunities to expose demonstrated high performers at an early stage in their professional lives to career defining positions. Consider the case of Colin Powell. He was first exposed to the highest levels of our government and some of the most influential American leaders of the day including Casper Weinberger and Frank Carlucci, two future secretaries of defense.

Other examples of potential capacity-enhancing positions for military officers outside of the normal chain of command could include assignment to the National Security Council staff, the Department of State, Department of Homeland Security, the Office of the National Drug Control Policy, Drug Enforcement Agency, or within the Intelligence Community. Likewise, assignment of a State Department Foreign Service officer to the Department of Defense early in his or her career would provide a great opportunity for immersion into a different culture and organization and to broaden one's perspective.

However, it is not enough to place promising performers into these broadening assignments. After completing a capacity building assignment, the individual must be tracked into and out of progressively more challenging assignments to ensure that he or she can make use of these experiences and also remain current in the mainstream of the organization. For example, if a mid-grade military officer is assigned to a position of the NSC staff, the goal should be for that officer to come back to the military and continue to assume roles of more and greater responsibility. These opportunities must not be considered to be poor choices for professional development. Rather they should be considered choice assignments. Likewise, only the most promising officers should be considered for these types of opportunities.

In addition to training, education, and experiences, mentorship is another key component for increasing the capacity of an individual. Mentorship amounts to being a counselor or guide to assist in the development of an individual. A mentor can be formal or informal depending on the degree to which the mentoring is directly supported by the organization. It can run the gamut from simple discussions to counseling or even assistance in guiding the career path of an individual. In the case of Eisenhower and his mentor, Gen. Fox Connor, Connor spent personal and professional time teaching and coaching Eisenhower as well as ensuring he received the correct developmental assignments, such as serving as an aide to the legendary General Pershing.

Equally important in the process of identifying and mentoring future strategic leaders is the identification of those individuals that have a terminal capacity below the strategic level. Whether due to character, training, experiences, or other reasons, some individuals will lack the capacity to serve at the highest levels of an organization.

The leader development process takes on urgency when one realizes that a future chairman of the Joint Chiefs of Staff is likely a lieutenant or ensign in the service today. Who is developing this future leader and ensuring the proper mix of training, education, experiences, and mentoring?

Identifying and developing the senior civilian leaders in our government in the area of security and defense is perhaps even more difficult. No career path exists for developing leaders such as the secretaries of defense, state, and homeland security; their deputies; or other senior political appointees.

Given the ambiguity and uncertain nature of the Information Age, can one really afford to have leaders that are not immediately prepared for the rigors of the position to which they are appointed? This appears to introduce unnecessary risk into the security and defense of our nation.

The National Security Personnel System (NSPS) should assist in putting capable individuals into key slots and then moving senior civilians to get a better mix of leaders in the senior positions within an administration.

And reaching down to the state and local levels, how do organizations train, educate, and mentor these officials in their new and emerging roles in the security and defense arena? These are questions and issues that beg for attention and twenty-first century; Information Age leaders must be the ones to address the needs.

CHAPTER 5

Three Big Ideas for U.S. National Leadership in the Information Age

To this point, the focus has been on defining leadership and examining how leadership and thus leaders must change for success in the Information Age. Unlike the previous discussions, this section develops themes for several key areas in which national leadership will be vital for enhancing America's security in this new era: (1) developing a new U.S. national security strategy for the Information Age, (2) establishing a system of national service, and (3) committing to a greater national investment in the promotion of the benefits of globalization.

On the surface, the reader might be tempted to question why these three initiatives were chosen and how they specifically relate to the globalized Information Age. What makes these more important than the other challenges facing America in this age of globalization?

First, the intention was to establish reach goals for improving our national security rather than attempting to make small, peripheral changes that are on the margin. It would be easy to look at the government's response to Hurricanes Katrina and Rita in summer 2005 and conclude that further changes are required for a more coordinated response capability. Some have suggested a larger federal role. Others want the Federal Emergency Management Agency (FEMA) taken out from under the control of the Department of Homeland Security (DHS). Indeed, it is possible to find nearly as many opinions on the subject as there are people purporting to have knowledge of the situation or a plan of action. The same can be said of efforts that are focused outside the United States. The Department of State has been working to stand up an office for stability and reconstruction since mid-2003. The Department of Defense is likewise redoubling efforts to improve stability operations capabilities and doctrine. Both efforts certainly have merit, but the real issue to be confronted is whether they should reside at the national level or remain nested within one or more of the cabinet-level departments.

Second, the changes to the global environment necessitate a new way of thinking about our national security. We must recognize and act with the understanding that the United States will benefit if the resultant opportunities from the Information Age are more equally spread throughout the world. The environment in which the United States finds itself today, both internally and externally, demands a serious redressing. Much of the instability around the globe in these early years of the twenty-first century relates directly to the globalization that is occurring. Unfortunately the prosperity and benefits sometimes associated with globalization are reaching peoples, societies, nations, and even entire regions at different rates—or not at all, in some cases. This leads to friction and instability, exacerbated by the ability of disenfranchised people to understand and sometimes act accordingly to change or respond to their conditions.

As these three "big ideas" for the Information Age are developed, the reader will undoubtedly find intersection and relationships between these recommendations. This is to be expected given that they are all related to enhancing America's security for future generations.

A New National Security for the Information Age

In *Securing America's Future: National Strategy in the Information Age*, the point is made that America must develop a new national security strategy for the Information Age. It is not that all of the foundations on which the U.S. national strategy is based have changed or somehow become irrelevant, but rather that they have changed enough such that a national commitment led by the executive branch with close collaboration with Congress and the Supreme Court must be undertaken as a matter of the utmost importance.

This top-to-bottom review must focus on how the elements of national power are currently being employed, which ones should be added to a broadened application of national security strategy, and what changes in policies, laws, and behaviors must be implemented.

If one considers that power can be used in foreign and domestic venues and can be divided into hard and soft power, this forms four distinct applications: hard power focused externally, soft power focused externally, hard power focused domestically, and soft power focused domestically.

Throughout the history of the United States, national security strategy has primarily amounted to the use of hard power focused externally. Since its birth as a nation, the United States has followed policies that allowed for the free and unencumbered flow of goods and services to the limits of what the markets and transportation systems would bear. We have focused vast resources on developing the political institutions, military capabilities, and intelligence apparatus that have contributed to the United States becoming a global power, overwhelming the Soviet Union and Warsaw Pact, and now in the post–Cold War period allowing us to attain the mantle of the world's only hyperpower.

This amounts to a narrowly focused application of strategy, using political, military, and intelligence capabilities focused on foreign nations. But what about the other three possibilities?

Why not incorporate economics, education, human rights, media and public diplomacy, health, science and technology, and the environment into our national security equation? The use of soft power in a foreign capacity can and must be targeted to promote a greater understanding of America and its ideals and values, promote global economic prosperity, and increase global well-being. America must also gain the cultural understanding to deal with the world on different terms. Our messages of peace, freedom, human rights, and economic prosperity would likely receive considerably more enthusiastic support if they were not wrapped in realpolitik and carried overseas by U.S. military forces with the message of democracy for all. Instead of selling democracy, which has become a lightning rod with many societies around the world, would we not be wiser to encourage the rule of law and economic prosperity? The spread of democratic institutions would be a natural outcome for nations that embraced these principles.

Consider the benefits that accrue from supporting better educational systems and policies in the developing world or in those nations that lack basic freedoms. Today the Department of Education has the charter for U.S. education. Should this be expanded to encourage better education overseas as part of our national security strategy? If the answer is yes, then more than just policy formulation must be required; real resources would need to flow to make a program such as this a reality.

What about the use of power, hard or soft, in a domestic setting to accomplish national security objectives? One half of the potential application of national power (that is, the use of hard and soft power domestically) requires considerably more thought and debate. The basic mistrust of the military dating back to the Founding Fathers formed the basic DNA of the Constitution, which has served to limit the use of the military within the boundaries of the United States.[1] Only special authorities such the Insurrection Act or, more recently, the Patriot Act have given more authority to the executive branch in times of crisis. On a normal basis, the use of the military in domestic situations is limited by *posse comitatus*—the Reconstruction-era law that prohibits federal troops from taking part in law-enforcement operations. The exception concerns the National Guard, which can be called out by the state governors to respond to emergencies under their Article 32 powers. The federalization of the National Guard under Title 10 requires presidential authority.

The debate about domestic spying since 9/11 that came to light in late 2005 demonstrates that great emotion is attached to the question of individual liberties and the use of military and other intrusive governmental programs within our nation's borders.

Certainly related to the need for a new national security strategy for the United States is the need for a comprehensive, end-to-end system for consequence management. The term "consequence management" refers to dealing with the effects a major catastrophic event on U.S. territory. Today national capabilities are based largely on disaster relief efforts and experiences resulting from 9/11. Since 9/11, significant resources have been devoted to improving in this critical area, but are we prepared?

In the aftermath of 9/11, the Department of Homeland Security has been established and Intelligence Community reorganized. The Department of Defense also established a new regional combatant command called Northern Command (NORTHCOM) with geographic responsibilities for the United States; key duties also require interface and coordination with the Department of Homeland Security as well as the rest of the "alphabet soup" of agencies responsible for pieces of defending and securing America. Unfortunately the creation of these structures was not accompanied by a comprehensive review of the government to identify and correct the seams that have been created or those that existed previously.

The debate that occurred in the aftermath of Hurricane Katrina was directly related to these authorities and the question of states' rights that was decided by the Continental Congress, memorialized in the Constitution and Bill of Rights, and fought over in the Civil War. Consider a series of questions that get at the heart of the issue. If the federal government was aware of a situation, either natural or manmade, that could threaten a local area, should the federal government provide warning? And if the warning goes unheeded by the local authorities, should there be a federal response, or should the U.S. government simply allow the state and local governments to deal with the consequences? And finally, at what point should the response be federalized?

Virtually all would agree that the federal government does have a role in providing warning. However, I also believe that the answer to the other two questions would not receive the same support. They are far more likely to be based on the severity of the situation and receive considerably more scrutiny. A catastrophe such as Katrina or the 9/11 terrorist attacks that overwhelms local response capabilities will likely cause more people to request a federal response, while the Ruby Ridge incident in northern Idaho in 1992, during which a weeklong standoff between white supremacist Randy Weaver and federal agents ended in a shootout in which an FBI sniper shot and killed Weaver's wife, Vicky, would not. The Ruby Ridge confrontation began a week earlier when federal marshals tried to arrest Weaver for failing to appear in court on weapons charges. At that time, a gun battle erupted between marshals and Weaver's fourteen-year-old son, resulting in the deaths of Weaver's son and a marshal. The latter scenario is more likely to be looked at as a local law enforcement issue rather than a federal issue, despite the fact that Weaver was wanted on a federal weapons charge. To complicate matters even more, what about a scenario such as occurred at Kent State in 1970, when National Guardsmen fired on protesters of the Vietnam War policies and killed four of the students? This scenario likely would result in even greater lack of clarity concerning the appropriateness of a federal response.

As an example of the reluctance of states to have the federal government assume greater responsibility for consequence management activities, consider the response to a *USA Today* survey in October 2005 in which state governors were asked to respond to President Bush's suggestion that the Pentagon could take the lead in responding to catastrophic natural disasters. Of the thirty-eight governors who responded, only two backed the idea.[2] Even the president's brother, Governor Jeb Bush of Florida, rejected the idea and emphasized that local authorities have the responsibility in disaster relief in an Op-Ed titled "Think Locally on Relief."[3]

If one considers recent experiences with catastrophic events, a consideration that should give our national, state, and local leaders cause for concern is that each event has resulted in a steep learning curve with several of the lessons being repeated between events. Consider the lessons collected as part of the 9/11 Commission Report dealing with first responders, communications capabilities, and necessary response equipment. Many of these same lessons were relearned or at least not corrected during response to Hurricane Katrina almost four years later. Additionally, we have not seen the even more demanding cases that are possible; the terrorist attacks of 9/11 were point targets confined to specific sites, while Katrina was a large area of devastation. What about a case where there are multiple large area targets or disaster sites requiring massive simultaneous relief efforts?

Like the leaders of sixty years ago in the post–World War II period, today's national leaders must recognize that America's security in the future will be based on the ability to adapt our system. Try to imagine fighting and managing the Cold War without the benefits of the National Security Act of 1947. The CIA would not exist, nor would the Department of the Air Force. The interagency process used to manage the post-war period would not have existed either. The institutions that served us so well in the

Cold War period must be examined with a fresh perspective considering the challenges and opportunities of the Information Age.

Some may argue that the establishment of the Department of Homeland Security and the reorganization of the Intelligence Community are equivalent to the reorganization that took place in the post–World War II period. The difference is subtle but important. The National Security Act of 1947 resulted from a holistic look at the national security of this nation. It was undertaken following an evaluation of the emerging threat and the strategic vision for the United States. The reorganizations following 9/11 were narrowly focused on subordinate elements of national security, homeland security, and intelligence. This is not to diminish the role of either of these stovepipe areas, but rather to gain recognition that we have failed to look at security as a system with all of its component parts rather than just two areas requiring reexamination. I therefore recommend a comprehensive review of the national security system and strategy of the United States; this would be far more appropriate given the magnitude of the changes in the environment and the ongoing globalization that is occurring.

Some might even argue that reconvening a second Continental Congress might be in order. Even the notion of doing this seems remote and fraught with danger. But consider that in Iraq, we expect the people to emerge from almost forty years of an authoritarian government, vote in free elections for the first time in the nation's history, and establish a constitution, all in a thirty-month period. Certainly a careful reexamination of our own foundations is in order and achievable. While I would stop short of demanding a new Continental Congress be convened, a more comprehensive review of our national security is necessary.

Several imperatives surface when developing an Information Age strategy for the United States. We must find a way to cast the network over all key departments, agencies, and responders at the federal, state, and local levels. This does not necessarily imply providing classified information down to these levels, but rather the right information by which to see the situation, understand the situation, act according to the situation, and accomplish the required tasks to finish decisively. If this sounds familiar, it should—it is part of the equation for the capacity required of future leaders.

A related task is ensuring that all necessary actors have the basics, including communications, self-protection equipment, and relief supplies. Equally important is the development of the procedures, policies, and actions that will be crucial to quick, even automatic, responses in the event of a national emergency. Exercises and coordination at all levels must be conducted and institutionalized.

Another imperative is understanding and in some cases developing the links among all the players in the national security arena. This exercise is far more than simply developing the organizational charts and aligning responsibilities. Inherent in this task is to determine how each of the elements interacts into a seamless national security system. At the heart of the development of a new national security strategy is the requirement for an increased role of the National Security Council (NSC). The NSC was established as a policy formulation organization with the interagency process as the means by which decisions were made and information passed back to individual actors for implementation. As an example in the Conventional Armed Forces in Europe (CFE) negotiations in the late 1980s, the NSC met frequently at the working group, deputy, and principal levels to consider various proposals, develop a consistent U.S. policy, and issue guidance to the negotiating team. This guidance was transmitted to the State Department and retransmitted to the team in Europe sitting at the negotiating table.

The responsibilities of the NSC must be expanded to allow for exercising operational direction. That does not necessarily mean a command relationship in a strict military sense, but rather the ability to issue operational directives. To put a fine point on the issue, consider operations in Iraq that began in 2003. The United States failed to take advantage of strategic windows of opportunity at critical points, in large measure because it lacked the national capability to project all of the elements of national power in a coordinated manner. While the accomplishment of the strict military tasks was fairly straightforward, especially in the early stages of the conflict from March through May 2003, the inability to follow with the full range of national capabilities hindered the accomplishment of the broader set of objectives and set the conditions for the growth of the insurgency that ensued. For a variety of reasons that will undoubtedly receive more scrutiny through the lens of history, the planning and execution of the follow-on missions to bring the basis of a functioning society to Iraq severely lagged behind the purely military tasks. Even some thirty months into the operation, little overall change to the basic services available to the average Iraqi had occurred, and the production of oil had actually decreased from the prewar production levels of 2.6 million to 1.9 million barrels a day as of October 2005.[4]

A fallout from this experience is that much of the burden for accomplishing the post-combat tasks has fallen to the military, which in many cases lack core competencies in areas such as establishing local governments, delivering basic services, oil production, and standing up societies. De facto, the military is functioning at a level above where it should and in some cases coordinating the national response rather than concentrating on the military tasks involving security and the training of Iraqi forces for foreign internal defense (FID). It is understandable that during the early phases of an operation, the military will be doing more non-military tasks before the other elements of power have been deployed and while the security situation is tenuous. However, after three years, it is not unreasonable to expect that the situation would be such that a robust deployment of the other departments into the theater would permit the military to revert to its more traditional roles. However, operations in Iraq indicate that in several areas the opposite is true. In September 2005, a report surfaced that stated, "The U.S. military plans to take over responsibility from the State Department for providing assistance to Iraq's Defense and Interior Ministries, following the determination that greater resources and expertise are needed."[5] The responsibility is going from the Iraq Reconstruction Management Office (IRMO) within the State Department to the Department of Defense. Perhaps most damning is that the article states that the State Department has been struggling to fill the slots where ten of fifty-one positions remain vacant. It is hard to fathom that for a mission of national importance, a nation of 300 million people cannot find ten individuals able to fill these critical slots.

We must also include state and local leaders in the developmental process. Governors and other key nonfederal leaders should be identified to participate. In this way, a new strategy can be conceived that will have the perspective of the recent consequence management events such as in the aftermath of 9/11 or Hurricane Katrina.

To add a final exclamation point on this argument, today the United States continues to rely on foundations established 230 years ago to defend against threats and respond to situations in the twenty-first century. Could the early leaders of the Republic really have envisioned the changes and challenges that we face today? Or is change, or at least consideration of change, in order? I think the answer is yes.

So what is our national strategy? And what should it be?

This is where national leadership becomes vital. National leaders in the executive, legislative, and judicial branches must work together to accomplish this comprehensive review of the security apparatus and develop strategies for advancing national interests and objectives. The fate of the American empire rests on the ability of leaders of character to come together in a nonpartisan environment to develop a new national security strategy. None of the branches working in isolation can achieve this great purpose.

The methodology to be used should be similar to the Base Realignment and Closure (BRAC) process. The initial step in this process was the development of criteria for assessing the military value of the bases held by the U.S. Armed Forces. Next was a determination of which bases could be divested from the perspective of military efficiency and effectiveness as well as economic impact to the surrounding communities. The final list was presented by the Department of Defense to the BRAC Commission (made up of nine specially selected commissioners), which then considered the submission, evaluated the impact of the recommendations, and made additions or deletions prior to submitting the final list to Congress for consideration of a single up-or-down vote. The BRAC recommendations were then forwarded to the White House for final approval. This methodology reduces the potential for political maneuvering and provides for a more coherent set of recommendations.

For a new national security strategy to be developed using a similar methodology, the initial step would be to identify key experts from across the interagency, Congress, and the judicial branch. These experts would have the mission to make recommendations for the redesign of the national security apparatus of the United States. The individuals would need to represent most of the major agencies and departments from across the government to include representatives from the state and local levels.

Finally, a comprehensive national security strategy for the Information Age and its implementation must account for the interests and objectives the country desires to achieve by providing the appropriate ways and means at an acceptable level of risk, subject of course to the environment in which we are executing our strategy. The result must be a new National Security Act of 20XX, related to its predecessor, the National Security Act of 1947, through the foundations and history of our nation.

Establishing a System of National Service

> Ask not what your country can do for you; ask what you can do for your country.
>
> —President John F. Kennedy[6]

We must develop and implement a system of national service that requires each citizen of the United States to bear some burden to support the society from which they benefit in a manner appropriate to their desires and skills. This in no way implies a return to the draft, but rather that each of us has a responsibility to serve our nation in some capacity. Some may choose to serve the nation in uniform, while perhaps others may decide to participate as volunteer police or fire fighters, legal aid specialists, emergency room technicians, doctors, volunteers for charities, and a host of other activities. Still others may opt for programs such as the Peace Corps or positions with nongovernmental organizations overseas or in the United States.

A system of national service must be considered to be more than just an important source of manpower for the nation, but also a key strategy for bringing Americans together, and allowing the United States to live up to its full potential as a world leader. Having a greater cross section of America trained in areas such as federal, state, and local security issues; disaster response; and humanitarian efforts, to name a few areas that could be targeted for service, would have both immediate benefits for society and our nation as well as long-term and perhaps less tangible benefits for communities and individuals.

The complexity of implementing such a system is not lost on the author, but that must be weighed against the enormous benefit to our communities, our society, and our nation. To attempt to "give credit" for service in a national system that may link paid and unpaid services will certainly be challenging, but also much needed in this new era.

Other challenges would undoubtedly include determining the length of service for each of the approved positions and the personal timelines for each individual. For example, a soldier joining the army normally enters as a seventeen- to twenty-four-year-old and remains in the army for a three-year enlistment, after which the Soldier can elect to remain in the service. An individual studying to become a doctor or lawyer would most likely not be available for national service until completion of his or her advanced degree and would be slightly older, although he or she could opt to perform national service concurrently based on personal preference. Depending on the type of national service rendered, the lawyer could potentially serve in a position for a shorter duration if it was full time, or perhaps over a longer period if the national service was part-time or on an as-needed basis.

What can be done to ensure that more individuals are capable of assisting in the security and defense of our nation? The key to implementation would be to match individual skills with national requirements subject to personal preferences to fill vital areas where today a vacuum exists. Consider the following examples for a system of national service (See Table 4). They are representative of the types of programs that should be established; certainly many other permutations are possible. Along with the listing of some potential programs are some of the benefits and costs provided by way of an overview.

Of course more traditional national service conducted as a primary profession such as serving full time in the military, police, first responders, or government employees to name a few could also be "count" as fulfilling the national service obligation. Individuals self-selecting into these full time positions would receive credit for national service. The requirement would be to have each American reaching majority participate in this system of service.

Table 4. Examples of National Service

Primary Position	National Service Position	Implementation
Store Manager	National Guard	Individual has a primary job in the civilian sector, but serves as a sergeant in the National Guard, which requires weekend and annual training. Receives pay according to rank in the military.
Doctor	Doctor	Works at a major hospital yet serves at a local clinic for four hours a week as a volunteer. Falls under the purview of Department of Health and Human Services.
College Professor/ Teacher	Linguist	Speaks French and Spanish fluently. In addition to primary position of teaching, is trained and available to provide services as an interpreter for the Department of State or the military. Is available for deployments targeted to the summer time frame, when school is out of session. Compensation based on time activated.
City Planner	Disaster Relief Team Leader	Based on experience in city planning, volunteers on a disaster relief team that could be "activated" for emergencies. In addition to training, particularly in relief planning, individual is on a roster of available people to be called up as necessary. Attends monthly planning meetings and is in a program of continuous self-education to remain current. Receives compensation for costs incurred and small stipend. Program administered by the DHS.
College Student	International Election Monitor	Either as part of the curriculum or during breaks, students could serve as election monitors as part of a United Nations election monitoring effort. Pre-deployment training would need to be conducted and pay for the period of service could be provided.

Why is a system such as this vital to America? Today we have a system of national security where a very small number of individuals provide for the national security of our nation. The uniformed military of two million people represents far less than one percent of the population. Even if one adds the Coast Guard and the first responders, including fire, police, medical, and other local civil servants dedicated to protecting society, the numbers are quite small compared to America's three hundred million total population. Furthermore, as Hurricane Katrina demonstrated when it slammed into the Gulf Coast in August 2005, many of the designated first responders were casualties themselves. It certainly would have been useful to have larger numbers of citizens in the affected region with experience and understanding of disaster relief operations and initial response capabilities. Thus by having a national service system, more Americans will be exposed to these types of capabilities and plans.

A significant benefit that cannot be overstated is the importance to the development and maintenance of a robust society related by more than proximity, but also a common sense of purpose and belonging; a system of national service would greatly contribute to the development of community.

Information technologies now allow for people who are "connected" to live, work, and play behind an electronic curtain. Today many employers permit telecommuting, which allows an employee to have a job without ever leaving the comfort of one's house. Shopping can also be done from home. Through the miracle of delivery services, meals, entertainment, and important papers can be brought right to the front doorstep or to the Internet portal. Most services have online help desks with Web-based customer service.

In many respects these capabilities free us from mundane tasks and allow for better use of time, but they have a downside as well. In the early years of the twenty-first century, it is possible to live as an electronic hermit with little or no contact with other humans other than through electronic devices. While somewhat counterintuitive, the capabilities associated with globalization made possible through enhancements in transportation and communications tend to both allow for increased interactions as well as isolate individuals from society. Thus as an increasingly large segment of the population chooses to retreat behind the computer screen, a significant drawback in the Information Age will be the impact on society as a whole.

A requirement for national service would draw those so inclined out of their electronic cocoons and force interactions with other humans for the express purpose of working for the common good on a project of national security (or at least local security).

An important benefit requiring more elaboration would be the exposure of much larger portions of society to the concept of national security. In the military we have developed that every soldier is a sensor on the battlefield. Each soldier is therefore trained in observing, evaluating, and reporting on situations that meet a set of commander's critical information requirements (CCIR). This information is determined by the commander to be of importance to the development of the situation and gaining an understanding of the environment. Using this same concept overlaid on a system of national service, a larger portion of the population could be trained to look for and report anomalies as they are observed. It follows that by better understanding national security and receiving training in these sorts of security issues, a greater number of "sensors" will be operating within our society.

The interactions through national service would also provide exposure to the government planning used in national security endeavors. Thus, an additional benefit would be to educate a broader cross section of America on security and response issues.

It is perhaps not too difficult to enumerate all the reasons why national service will not work, would be too costly, or other reasons for not implementing such a system. In the end, I believe it comes down to how to best involve more citizens in the business of national security, reach a broader cross section of society, and build a sense of community, while helping to offset some of the negatives associated with globalization and the Information Age. But make no mistake, it will come down to the commitment and energy of national leaders willing to push outside of traditional comfort areas and think differently about what it means to be part of a society such as we enjoy in America.

Committing to a Greater National Investment in the Promotion of the International Benefits of Globalization

Global interactions, promoted and accelerated by enhancements in communications and transportation since the beginning of the Industrial Age, have continued at an ever-increasing pace. With the advent of enhanced communications brought about through the Internet, the rate of global interaction, better known as globalization, has increased dramatically, driven by Moore's Law, which was first articulated by Gordon Moore from Intel Corporation. He observed that the number of transistors per square inch on integrated circuits had doubled every year since the integrated circuit was invented. Moore predicted that this trend would continue for the foreseeable future. In subsequent years, the pace slowed down a bit, but data density has doubled approximately every eighteen months, and this is the current definition of Moore's Law, which Moore himself has blessed. Most experts, including Moore himself, expect Moore's Law to hold for at least another two decades.[7]

If one thinks about the development of a global society from 1960 to perhaps 2050, enormous changes in the world will have occurred, promoting interaction between people, states, and societies. Consider the global transportation system using an example from North America.[8] In 1960 the North American population of 204 million traveled 5.5 trillion passenger-kilometers (pkm) by railways, buses, automobiles, and high-speed transport. By 2050, the projected North American population of 438 million will travel 103 trillion pkm. While the population experiences a 114 percent increase, the travel metric will increase by over 1,770 percent. The comparisons are even more distinct in the field of communications, particularly with regard to Internet communications. In 1960, the network was in early concept design stages. Many homes had telephones, but cellular telephones did not exist. Today, voice and data connectivity is considered ordinary throughout the industrialized areas of the world. Even in areas the Industrial and Information Ages have seemingly passed by or only slightly touched, evidence of connectivity can be found. I remember traveling in a fairly remote location in Latin America and seeing the local population carrying cellular telephones while tending to their livestock and traveling along unpaved roads. In these same areas, one could see satellite television dishes attached to nearly every dwelling, as if required by building codes.

Given that the world is becoming increasingly more connected and interdependent, what type of world do we want? What is or should be the

U.S. role in global development? Should the United States shape the outcome or simply employ a laissez-faire approach to allow for haphazard development and globalization? History provides some interesting data points for use in considering these weighty questions.

In the aftermath of World War I, President Woodrow Wilson proposed the establishment of an international forum for discussing world events, cooperating on relevant events of the day, and resolving potential conflicts. Given both the human and monetary cost of the war, it should come as no surprise that world leaders sought a remedy to ensure that a catastrophe of this magnitude would not occur in the future. Many prominent world leaders advocated a society of nations for promotion of international peace and security. Advocates believed that a forum for resolving conflict and dealing with issues of the day was essential. To this end, the League of Nations was established in 1919 at the Paris Peace Conference by the treaties that effectively ended the war. President Wilson incorporated provisions for establishing the League of Nations into his Fourteen Points, with a specific charter of promoting arbitration for settling international disputes; to bring about reduction of armaments; to study and remove the causes of war; and to promote world interests in all fields of human work.[9]

The potential for the League of Nations as an international forum for resolving conflict and addressing issues was demonstrated successfully during several tense standoffs during the interwar years.[10] However, despite some clear successes, the limitations of the League were perhaps even more noteworthy. In particular, the League of Nations lacked the ability to enforce decisions or police non-compliant nations. In a harbinger of events to unfold, in 1933, Germany withdrew from the League of Nations and began remilitarizing. From the outset, the credibility and thus the long-term viability of the League of Nations suffered a serious setback when the U.S. Senate refused to ratify the Treaty of Versailles, thus preventing the United States from taking a leadership role in this fledgling organization.

Despite the failure of the League of Nations to prevent World War II, one must give credit to Wilson for his creativity and personal investment in an endeavor such as this. Prior to its establishment, the balance of power system was maintained through a series of bilateral and modest multilateral treaties that limited specific behaviors or created alliances. The League of Nations was intended to be a global forum providing all signatories the opportunity to meet and discuss important international issues.

Following World War II, another U.S. president made a bold and calculated leadership move. President Franklin Roosevelt proposed the establishment of the United Nations. A significant lesson resulting from World War I was essentially relearned with the initiation of hostilities in World War II, the essentiality of an international forum for facilitating discussions between nations, maintaining order and discipline within the state system, resolving disagreements, and if necessary policing nations not in compliance with international laws. At the end of hostilities, representatives from fifty nations met in San Francisco in October 1945 to create the United Nations Charter. By the end of the conference, representatives from all fifty attending nations signed the charter; Poland, which was not represented at the conference, later signed as the fifty-first member nation. Today, the United Nations has a membership of over 190 nations.

Officially, the stated goals of the United Nations are: to maintain international peace and security; to develop friendly relations among nations based on respect for the principle of equal rights and self-determination of peoples; to cooperate in solving international economic, social, cultural, and humanitarian problems and in promoting respect for human rights and fundamental freedoms; and to be a center for harmonizing the actions of nations in attaining these common ends.

In the later decades of the twentieth century, the United Nations came under increasing criticism from a number of sides. Many of the criticisms, from mismanagement of resources to ineffective implementation of programs, have a degree of validity, but perhaps the more relevant question is whether there is a better system.

Many have criticized the UN's ability to enforce mandates, international laws, and agreements. The UN has sponsored fifty-nine peacekeeping operations since 1948, including sixteen that were ongoing as of December 2004 and that included almost 64,000 military personnel and civilian police. This list of fifty-nine consists of some that have received considerable scrutiny and harsh reviews, including Operation Restore Hope in Somalia and UN Protection Force (UNPROFOR) in Bosnia, which has garnered considerable criticism for its inability to stem the violence and restore order. Still, a UN mandate is in some respects considered by many nations to be a prerequisite prior to the employment of force for conflict resolution or to resolve differences.

The United States has argued that a disproportionate share of the funding for the United Nations is borne by America. It is true that the United States pays approximately one-third of the total assessment, and for some time was approximately $1 billion in arrears, based on a dispute over how the national assessments were developed.

Perhaps the most significant criticism facing the United Nations today is the lack of satisfaction in the power-sharing arrangements of the member nations. The larger nations believe that the one-country, one-vote formulation gives the smaller countries an equal and thus disproportionate voice in deciding outcomes. Thus a vote by Senegal carries as much weight in the General Assembly as a vote by the United States. Furthermore, a popular vote through the General Assembly to support a peacekeeping mission will cost the United States a third of the total cost based on the assessment process, regardless of whether the United States supports the operation.

Another issue of concern is the composition of the Security Council. The Security Council has fifteen members, five permanent members and ten elected by the General Assembly for two-year terms. The members of the Security Council, in particular the five permanent members—China, France, the Russian Federation, the United Kingdom, and the United States—are seen as having a disproportionate say in the affairs of United Nations. For example, there are those that believe they have claims to a permanent seat by virtue of population, economic capacity, military capability, or perhaps some other attribute. Notice that several major nations, such as India with a population of over one billion people, almost 17 percent of the world's total population, do not have permanent member status. Nor is there a Muslim country as a permanent member, despite the fact that the Muslim community represents approximately 20 percent of the world's population. In fact, the only two countries with large Muslim populations on the Security Council as of 2005 were Algeria and the Philippines.[11] Their terms both expired at the end of their two-year tenure. Qatar is currently a member through 2007.

An examination using economic well-being as an indicator also provides insights that are worthy of consideration. The total gross world product is $55.5 billion while the United States has a gross domestic product of $11.75 billion in 2004 dollars, or approximately 20 percent of the total. However, when one considers the population of the world versus the United States, 6.45 billion versus 300 million, it translates to 4.65 percent of the world's population having 20 percent of the economic clout. This simple analysis certainly provides a different perspective for considering how the United States might begin to look from the water's edge inward to the rest of the world.

Of course in considering the question of globalization and what America has done to support the spread of economic prosperity, rule of law, and democratic institutions, one must also look at initiatives such as those implemented through the World Bank and the International Monetary Fund (IMF) since these initiatives are directly related to the establishment of the United Nations and were championed by the United States.

The World Bank and IMF work in tandem in the developing world. The first IMF and World Bank meeting was held in July 1944, in Bretton Woods, New Hampshire. This meeting served as the economic component associated with the establishment of the United Nations. The UN came into existence in October 1945, and the Articles of Agreement were signed in December 1945. The next year, the bylaws were adopted at a meeting in Savannah, Georgia, in March 1946. The Bretton Woods agreement established stable yet adjustable exchange rates for the various currencies of the signatory nations. The value of the various national currencies was set to the dollar as the standard. Of course, the agreement also required the signatory nations to give up a degree of sovereignty with regard to setting national monetary policies. In the 1960s, pressures developed that culminated in the collapse of the Bretton Woods system in 1971 and replacement with a regime of floating exchange rates.

The goals of the World Bank are the elimination of poverty and the growth of sustained development. In the words of the World Bank, it assists developing countries by "building the climate for investment, jobs, and sustainable growth, so that economies will grow, and by investing in and empowering poor people to participate in development."[12]

The IMF was established as an international organization to promote international monetary cooperation, exchange stability, and orderly exchange arrangements; to foster economic growth and high levels of employment; and to provide temporary financial assistance to countries to help ease balance of payments adjustment. Since the IMF was established, its purposes have remained unchanged, but its operations—which involve surveillance, technical assistance, and financial assistance—have developed to meet the changing needs of its member countries in an evolving world economy. The IMF began in 1945 with less than fifty member nations and has grown to 184 member nations today.

The United States Agency for International Development (USAID) and recent agreements that have expanded free trade and the increased the potential for economic development also demonstrate programs undertaken by the United States to promote economic prosperity and long-term development, including promoting the spread of the positive aspects of globalization.

USAID provides assistance including technical assistance and capacity building, training and scholarships, food aid and disaster relief, infrastructure construction, small-enterprise loans, budget support, enterprise funds, and credit guarantees. Spending less than one-half of one percent of the federal budget, USAID works around the world to achieve these goals. USAID has working relationships, through contracts and grant agreements, with more than thirty-five hundred companies and over three hundred U.S.-based private voluntary organizations.[13]

The total obligations and loans for 2003 were $31.6 billion, representing over a 50 percent increase over the 2002 program of $20.9 billion. The spending data is further subdivided into economic assistance and military assistance. For 2003, the $31.6 billion is divided into $19.9 billion in economic and $11.7 billion in military aid.

Of course, these USAID totals do not include private contributions given to nongovernmental organizations or those given in the aftermath of natural disasters such as the tsunami in December 2004, killing an estimated three hundred thousand people in the Indian Ocean region, impacting twelve nations, and displacing several million other people.

Still, it is worth making the point that in 2005, the United States spent well over half a trillion dollars in military spending while only slightly more than $20 billion for economic assistance through our principal aid dispensing organization; that equates to spending only about 4 percent on global economic development and prosperity, or twenty-five times more on defense. Note that this only really accounts for the Department of Defense's share of security and defense and does not account to the resources allocated to the Department of Homeland Security or by state and local authorities.

The North American Free Trade Agreement (NAFTA) and the more recently proposed, yet not currently in effect, Central American–Dominican Republic Free Trade Agreement (CAFTA-DR) represent additional tools that have been or could be employed in the fight against poverty and the promotion of regional development. NAFTA was signed in 1994 by Canada, Mexico, and the United States for the promotion of economic growth and raising the standards of living in all three nations. At the time of its signing, it represented the largest free trade area in the world. It continues to retain this title even after the recent expansion of the European Union (EU) to twenty-five nations.

The U.S. Congress approved CAFTA-DR in July 2005, and the president signed it into law on August 2. CAFTA-DR has been approved by the legislatures in El Salvador, Guatemala, and Honduras; approval is pending in Costa Rica, the Dominican Republic, and Nicaragua. The official website of the U.S. Department of Commerce states, "Once implemented, U.S. manufacturers, workers, farmers, and ranchers will benefit from its market opening provisions."[14]

Despite the potential for promoting growth within regions that are on America's doorstep, both NAFTA, which is in effect, and CAFTA–DR, which has yet to enter into force, have detractors within the United States who are adamantly opposed to these sorts of free trade agreements.

In a very real sense, all the programs discussed above, from the League of Nations at the end of the First World War to the NATFA and CAFTA-DR agreements, represent efforts to manage globalization through the spread of economic prosperity. Of course, the cynic could make the countercase that these initiatives were really veiled attempts to remake the world in America's image and to give America the upper hand in global competition. I would like to believe that the former is the case and thus take an idealistic view of America's motivations.

In addition to the issues of power sharing, the competence to conduct missions, and the ability to enforce decisions, the United Nations is also dealing with the complex issues associated with an increasingly interconnected and globalized world and the tensions that will undoubtedly ensue. Issues such as the spread of poverty, lack of education, malnutrition, HIV/AIDS, the potential for a pandemic Asian bird flu virus, environmental degradation including the spread of greenhouse gases, manmade conflict and famine, terrorism, proliferation of weapons and nuclear technology, women's rights and human rights more generally, and ethnic strife are just a small subset of the global issues to be addressed and alleviated. An interesting exercise would be to ask the member nations to rank this list from issues of most to least concern. Could the over 190 members come anywhere close to reaching a consensus on the final ranked list? And are issues such as HIV/AIDS or the pandemic Asian bird flu really national security issues?

An example describing the Black Death illustrates the potentially destructive nature of transnational threats that may not have catastrophic implications on U.S. national security. A Council on Foreign Relations special report entitled "HIV and National Security: Where Are the Links?" demonstrates the impact of the plague in Europe:

> When the Yersinia pestis bacterium hit Europe in the fall of 1347, no one at the time could imagine that the mysterious pestilence would challenge the integrity of city-states, turn the continent's economy on its head, and set the surviving populace on a course that would lead to the collapse of feudalism and the rise of the Protestant Reformation.[15]

Other key outcomes included the elimination of adults aged twenty to sixty years, disruptions in the lineages of societies, widespread poverty, and increased political instability, which eventually led to political change in Europe.

Today many believe we are seeing the early stages of another equally disconcerting trend in the spread of disease. Consider the impact that HIV/AIDS is having around the world; forty million people are estimated to be infected as of 2004, with over twenty-five million in Africa alone. Imagine the implications if drug-resistant strains continue to proliferate or if the means of transmission adapts to become other than invasive contact such as through sexual contact, intravenous drug use, or blood transfusions. What happens if the virus mutates and goes airborne? Then whose problem will it be? The answer is clear. With increased migration and contact between societies, what happens in Africa is indeed very likely to affect our national security.

So now let's look at the questions again in light of the previous historical examples. Given that the world is becoming increasingly more connected and interdependent, what type of world is desirable? What is or should be the U.S. role in global development? Should we shape the outcome or simply employ a laissez-faire approach to allow for haphazard development and globalization?

America's leaders must make a concerted effort to afford the benefits of globalization across the globe. To do anything less places our long-term national security in jeopardy. We must continue with the efforts to manage globalization to ensure that its benefits are available to an increasingly greater percentage of the world's population. It is not possible for America to build robust enough defenses to defend and secure America against all threats. We must follow the leadership of Wilson and Roosevelt to search for a better world in which America will continue to lead and thrive.

This section has explored committing to a great national investment in the promotion of the international benefits of globalizations. However, this commitment does not necessarily entail a fiscal commitment alone or even primarily. Global policies can and must be adjusted to eliminate barriers to economic development.

This chapter has presented three "big ideas" requiring U.S. leadership in the Information Age: developing a new national security strategy for the United States, establishing a system of national service, and promoting the international benefits of globalization. These three were chosen because I believe that they represent the biggest challenges to the United States. Each will require a concerted effort from determined leaders of wisdom.

In chapter 4, four key areas were identified as placing a greater demand on the twenty-first-century leader: vision and communication, analysis and judgment, perspective, and the three Is—imagination, innovation, and initiative.

By way of an exercise, place yourself in the position of a national leader attempting to implement one of the three "big ideas." If you were the president, how would you utilize these key components to gain support for your proposals? What if you were a member of the Congress?

Imagine the difficulty associated with developing a new national security strategy for the United States. I am not talking about the publication every four years of the *National Security Strategy of the United States* by the White House, but rather of a new strategy like the strategy of containment developed by George Kennan and first articulated in an article in *Foreign Affairs* in 1947. Not only would a healthy dose of vision be required in crafting such a new strategy, but likely every ounce of effort that could be mustered would be required to communicate the new strategy.

Perhaps an even greater effort would be required to communicate the need for America to commit to greater support for promoting the international benefits of globalization. In developing such a strategy, great empathy and perspective would be required to understand the need to balance the ways and means so as not to overwhelm or control, but rather support those nations affected. Overwhelming or attempting to control would be more likely to cause adverse reactions and repercussions while appropriate levels of support are far more likely to lead the proliferation of the benefits of globalization.

In some regards, implementing a system of national service may place the greatest demands on our leaders and the country. All four of the key areas of twenty-first-century leadership would be essential in the development, promotion, and support of such a program. As with all things new and different, there would be a period of adaptation and adjustment. In the end, the benefits for individuals, communities, our society, and our nation would far outweigh these short-term issues.

CHAPTER 6

Conclusions

Throughout the developed and developing world, the Information Age is upon us and touching virtually all areas of our lives. Changes fueled by information technologies will continue to impact, both positively and negatively, our lives, and globalization will continue at an ever increasing pace. We cannot stop globalization, even if we desired to do so; the genie is out of the bottle. Therefore, we must develop mechanisms to maximize the opportunities and mitigate the challenges. This is where strong, unencumbered leaders of character will be vital to the future of America.

The free flow of data will require that societies, organization, individuals, and leaders work together to maximize the potential of this new era. Advances in traditional fields including manufacturing, design medicine, and services will be affected as will new and emerging fields such as biotechnology, robotics, and networking. Things thought to be impossible will become mundane in the Information Age. Vast amounts of information will be available for the harvesting and the world will be more connected and less isolated. Security of information will become more and more important as systems and individuals with the knowledge to access and probe networks continue to grow. New relationships will form and old ones may be placed in jeopardy; the ideological tectonic plates will shift and alliances will be adjusted in response.

As we look to the future, we must be mindful of the growing body of threats and challenges that will confront the United States in the Information Age. Future conflict will be less about the physical domain and more about the competition for ideas. We must be prepared for this new type of competition. We should not be surprised to see that in the early years of this new century others, including our competitors and potential adversaries, are developing Information Age capabilities and leaders. This should not come as a surprise as few, if any will attempt to match our capabilities one-for-one. Rather they will change the playing field to accommodate their strengths. If we are playing soccer, they will play tennis. When we change to tennis, they will switch to rugby. We must be prepared across the spectrum of conflict.

What this means in practical terms is that we must understand and internalize what it means to compete in a conflict of ideas. To succeed in this environment, we cannot hope to realistically match military forces against ideas and hope to win. We must develop the insights, capabilities, and perseverance to compete and win in this new way of waging modern war. Furthermore, to be successful, we cannot hope to fight a purely reactive strategy. We must seize the initiative in the competition for ideas now, even with friendly competitors. This must be done before escalation into conflict in the other domains. Perhaps at no time in history has it been truer that the early stages of the next conflict are being waged today in many nontraditional forums.

We must also learn to "fight" on multiple levels simultaneously. Today we are fighting complex insurgencies in Iraq and Afghanistan within the physical, social, cognitive, and information domains. We are winning in some of the domains and losing in others. To be successful, we must master multiple domains in a single conflict to arrive at true Information Age warfare.

Equally important are the conflicts in other regions of the world, such as in Indonesia and Pakistan, that are fought less in the physical domain and more in the social, cognitive, and information domains in the competition for ideas within the Muslim world. We must also remain keenly focused on the other competitive environments, such as with China or in the countries that dominate the oil producing nations of the world. And in our future constructs, we cannot just focus on states and nations, but also on transnational actors and the free flows of ideas and thoughts.

All this leads to one important conclusion regarding the Information Age leader of tomorrow. We must develop leaders of character and capabilities that are up to the challenges of the twenty-first century.

Information Age leaders will have greater rather than fewer requirements for leadership capabilities in this new era. It may seem counterintuitive that with increases in automation, a corresponding decrease in leader workload will not be gained, but with vast, more complex demands placed on leaders for building a personal repository of data, information, knowledge, and wisdom, while still maintaining the more traditional aspects of leadership, it stands to reason that the leader will have a greater range of personal requirements to satisfy.

The field of national security and defense will not be exempt from the requirement to develop Information Age capabilities grounded in the leadership traits and theories of the past while reaching for the future. The legacy left by the leaders of yesterday will be important as the foundation from which to develop this new brand of American Information Age leader. The wisdom of George Washington, who believed in setting high goals and having a vision for the future and setting an example, will still be important. The same holds true for Abraham Lincoln, who spoke of persuading rather than coercing, setting goals and being result-oriented, and encouraging innovation. The coalition-building capabilities of Dwight Eisenhower and the importance of mentors in developing Eisenhower into one of the great leaders of World War II also provide examples of important traits for the twenty-first-century leader.

As we look into the twenty-first century and what will be required of the Information Age leader, several key thoughts emerge. The leader must master the basic tenets of leadership and learn how to incorporate the imperatives for the Information Age: vision and communication, analysis and judgment, perspective, and the three I's (imagination, innovation, and initiative).

The foundations of leadership will remain the essential building block for the leader. But after the foundations, the ability of the leader to develop clear, unambiguous, and well-conceived strategies with a vision for the endstate and the capability to communicate this vision will be the single most important demand on the Information Age leader.

One might be a visionary with the greatest strategies, but failing to communicate them effectively will hamper their utility. More pointedly, a strategy with no communication is doomed to fail. In the same light, a terrible strategy failing to combine the *ways* and *means* into meaningful formulations with inappropriate or infeasible *ends*, perhaps even high *risk*, that is well communicated also fails to achieve the desired outcome and thus is more wishful thinking or illusion than a viable strategy. Vision and communication must go hand in hand. Remember the example of the farmer and his sons. It takes both vision and consistency in execution to have a viable strategy.

Another characteristic of the Information Age is that more will be demanded of leaders at increasingly lower levels. Because of the compression of levels with the field of strategy where more junior and less experienced people within the national security apparatus will have the ability to impact at the operational and strategic levels, the tactical levels of command must have more understanding and comprehension of the commander's vision and intent to allow for rapidly responding to the challenges and opportunities that will emerge. The junior leader cannot be expected to gain approval for every variation in plans prior to execution and still take advantage of all the opportunities that will become available or avoid potential risks if any and all changes to the original planning require approval and explanation. This is where the concept of commander's intent becomes so invaluable. The junior leader steeped in the commander's intent can make split-second decisions that are within the intent developed by the commander. Thus only actions outside of intent would require special approval from higher headquarters. Consider Eisenhower's use of the intent statement for the invasion of Europe in World War II. He gave clear mission orders and allowed senior commanders to execute within his broadly developed guidance.

Along with this requirement for lower levels to have greater strategic insight, an additional requirement exists to gain higher degree of comfort with uncertainty and ambiguity. This includes development of a personal toolkit for managing the new complexities of the Information Age. Just as

Malcolm Gladwell presents in *Blink*, the twenty-first-century leader must develop the requisite skills and body of knowledge to allow for this type of perceptive analysis and decision making. The Information Age leader must also have a set of tools for sorting through the virtual stacks of data available and be able to process and refine the data into useable information, knowledge, and wisdom.

National security leaders must learn to adjust *ways* and *means* in real-time to respond to *environmental* changes to reduce *risk* and ensure accomplishment of the *ends*. A rigid adherence to the application of *ways* and *means* during execution will likely fail to capitalize on the opportunities or avoid the pitfalls that present themselves during execution.

Gaining a true perspective of the environment and the competitor will also take on more importance in the Information Age. Developing a single perspective strategy will likely result in a lopsided formulation with little or no chance for success. The leader must understand that the nation, group, and society on which the strategy is being employed get a vote. Thus, they have an equal place in the consideration and development of a strategy.

The leader must be able to place himself or herself into the enemy's position and see the strategy through this perspective to assume great advantages toward the development of a successful set of goals and objectives.

Finally in the Information Age, the leader who takes maximum advantage of the three Is—imagination, innovation, and initiative—will have an enormous strategic benefit. A practical strategy, with great predictability and little imagination, will also have predictability from the adversary's standpoint allowing for counters to be developed and employed. Imagination is the antidote.

Innovation, which runs the gamut from gaining greater efficiency and effectiveness in current processes to creative solutions, must be incorporated into emerging-age strategies. The Information Age will allow for combining technologies, concepts, and ideas in various ways unlike at any time in history. The strategic leader must have the creativity and wisdom to embrace new and innovative solutions.

Initiative, especially in thinking and action, will also contribute to the strategic equation. Strategic leaders unafraid to make decisions, assume risk, and force the action will be vital. Empowered junior leaders with the understanding of the situation, the commander's intent, and the adversary's capabilities and intent will be able to make rapid decisions and show coherence in thought that will be imperative for winning the war of ideas.

With the emerging requirements of the Information Age, the strategic leader for America must be selected to with a keen eye toward maximizing the potential for success. This implies formal systems of training, education, experience, and mentorship as well as a selection system that identifies those with the inherent capacity for higher-level leadership and strategic thought. Whereas control measures were employed in the pre-Information Age period, these same measures would hamper the rapid decision making process.

A new environment mandates a new type of leadership. Just as the case was made for a new national security strategy for the Information Age, a parallel case for a new type of leader for the Information Age is developed. It will not be possible or even advisable to attempt to develop a set of scenarios for every type of contingency that could occur in the development and execution of strategy in this unpredictable environment, but we can develop the conceptual underpinnings to support how we will operate as a nation. This is where the break from the Industrial Age way of conducting strategy will occur.

In America today, many of the capabilities exist for leadership in the Information Age. The ability to harness these elements will depend on the willingness to look beyond the here and now. It will also require some fundamental departures from some of the internal politics that have driven America in the past. The adversary of tomorrow will be pleased to allow America to debate and argue internally while seeking to exploit the seams that exist.

Recently, a topic of great debate concerns the future of the American empire. Many wonder if America's best days are behind us. Will we fall prey to the failings of other empires such as the Roman, Byzantine, or Ottoman? These are important questions with very complex and perhaps even indefinable answers.

I believe that leaders, great Americans of character and capacity, with the legacy of the generations that have led the way, will be the key to securing America's future in the Information Age. The time for developing the future strategic leaders of America is now.

Notes

Preface

1. http://www.defenselink.mil/pubs/china.html.
2. From the Transformation Office from Office of the Secretary of Defense (OSD).
3. Robert L. Taylor and William E. Rosenbach, eds., *Military Leadership* (Boulder, CO: Westview Press, 1996), 206.
4. Ibid.

Chapter 1: Strategy and Leadership

1. *Encarta Dictionary, Encarta Encyclopedia* (online version). CD-ROM. Microsoft Corporation. http://encarta.msn.com/encyclopedia_1741588397/Globalization.html (accessed May 6, 2005).
2. Max Boot, unpublished manuscript (Council on Foreign Relations). Sources cited include Trevor N. Dupuy, *The Evolution of Weapons and Warfare* (Fairfax, VA: Hero Books, 1984), 310; all figures on lethality and dispersion up to 1973 are from Dupuy, *Evolution of Weapons*, 312. The figure for the Gulf War comes from Michael Russell Rip and James Michael Hasik, *The Precision Revolution* (Annapolis: Naval Institute Press, 2002), 126.
3. U.S. Department of the Army, *Information Operations: Doctrine Tactics, Techniques, and Procedures,* Field Manual 3-13 (FM 100-6) (Washington, DC: U.S. Government Printing Office, 2003), 2-1.
4. Data was compiled from Richard F. Grimmett, "The Instances of Use of United States Armed Forces Abroad, 1798–2001" (Washington, DC: Congressional Research Service, the Library of Congress), http://www.oft.osd.mil/ (updated February 5, 2002).
5. U.S. Department of the Army daily briefing, August 2, 2005, slide 3.

Chapter 2: Lists of Lists

1. U.S. Department of the Army, *Army Leadership,* Field Manual 22-100 (Washington, DC: GPO, 1999), 1-4.
2. Donald Clark, *Concepts of Leadership*, http://www.nwlink.com/~donclark/leader/leadcon.html (accessed May 1997).
3. M. E. Doyle and M. K Smith, "Classical Leadership," *Encyclopedia of Informal Education,* http://www.infed.org/leadership/traditional_leadership.htm (accessed July 24, 2006).
4. John Gardner, *On Leadership* (New York: Free Press, 1989).
5. James M. Kouzes and Barry Z. Posner, *The Leadership Challenge* (San Francisco: Jossey-Bass, 1987).
6. U.S. Department of the Army, *Military Leadership,* Field Manual 22-100 (Washington, DC: GPO, 1973).
7. U.S. Department of the Army, *Leadership and Command at Senior Levels,* Field Manual 22-103 (Washington, DC: GPO, 1987), 39.
8. Warren Bennis, *On Becoming a Leader* (Cambridge, MA: Basic Books, 2003), 39–40.
9. Robert R. Blake and Janse S. Mouton, *The Managerial Grid III: The Key to Leadership Excellence* (Houston: Gulf Publishing Co., 1985).
10. M. E. Doyle and M. K. Smith, "Classical Leadership," *The Encyclopedia of Informal Education,* http://www.infed.org/leadership/traditional_leadership.htm (accessed September 2001).
11. Sun Tzu, *The Art of War,* ed. James Clavell (New York: Delacorte Press, 1983), 9.
12. Ibid.
13. Ibid.
14. Ibid., 14.
15. Ibid., 16.
16. Ibid.
17. Ibid., 21.
18. Ibid., 11.
19. Ibid., 25.
20. Carl von Clausewitz, *On War*, trans. and ed. Michael Howard and Peter Paret (Princeton, NJ: Princeton University Press, 1984), 100.
21. Ibid., 102.

22. Ibid., 111.
23. Philip E. Schoenberg, "George Washington on Leadership," http://www.presidentialexpert.com/leadership_george_washington.html (accessed 2005).
24. Ibid.
25. Donald T. Phillips, *Lincoln on Leadership* (New York: Warner Business Book, 1992).
26. Ibid., back cover.
27. Richard M. McMurry, "Ole Joe in Virginia," in *Leadership and Command in the American Civil War,* ed. Steven E. Woodworth (El Dorado Hills, CA: Savas Woodbury Publishers, 1996), 23.
28. Philip E. Schoenberg, "Ulysses S. Grant on Leadership," http://www.presidentialexpert.com/leadership_ulysses_s_grant.html (accessed 2005).
29. Lesley J. Gordon, "Pickett After Gettysburg," in *Leadership and Command in the American Civil War,* 174.
30. Schoenberg, "Ulysses S. Grant on Leadership."
31. The White House, "Ulysses S. Grant," http://www.whitehouse.gov/history/presidents/ug18.html.
32. Philip E. Schoenberg, "Dwight D. Eisenhower on Leadership," http://www.presidentialexpert.com/leadership_dwight_d_eisenhower.html (accessed 2005).
33. The National Security Act of 1947 was established to coordinate foreign and defense policy. This legislation was revolutionary, as it formally established the structure for coordinating and implementing national security strategy. Key outcomes included creating a National Security Council (NSC), chaired by the president and including the secretaries of defense and state; establishing the Department of Defense and delineating the roles and responsibilities of the secretary of defense and staff; establishing the chairman of the Joint Chiefs of Staff and his staff, and the roles and responsibilities of the services; and developing a national intelligence structure, including the Central Intelligence Agency. Another important outcome was establishing a Department of the Air Force and keeping it a separate service of the Armed Forces.

34. Ronald Reagan, "Quotes: Leadership," online reference http://www.reaganfoundation.org/reagan/quotes/leadership.asp.
35. Frank Carlucci also served as a secretary of defense under President Ronald Reagan.
36. Colin Powell with Joseph E. Persico, *My American Journey* (New York: Random House, 1995), 613.
37. Elliott Jacques and Stephen D. Clement, *Executive Leadership: A Practical Guide to Managing Complexity* (Falls Church, VA: Cason Hall and Co. Publisher, 1991).
38. U.S. Department of the Army, *Army Leadership,* Field Manual 22-100 (Washington, DC: GPO, 1999), 1-4.

Chapter 3: Globalization and the Information Age

1. The term 20XX is used to signify that a future strategy, yet to be written, must be produced. Just as the National Security Act of 1947 indicates the development of the strategy in 1947, the National Security Act of 20XX indicates that the strategy would be developed in the twenty-first century.
2. U.S. Budget, Office of Management and Budget, The White House, Washington, DC, 2006.
3. Description of the "three-block war" is from Daniel M. Gerstein, *Securing America's Future: National Strategy in the Information Age* (Westport, CT: Praeger Security International, 2005), 33.
4. From a published undated pamphlet from the Office of the Secretary of Defense.
5. Ibid., 20–21.
6. Commander's intent is a military concept in which the leader specifies the purpose, method, and endstate for the action to be taken. In the case of a battle plan, the *purpose* contains the objective to be achieved, the *method* describes how the action will precede toward the objective, and the *endstate* describes what the environment will look like following the action.
7. The principles of war are mass, objective, security, surprise, maneuver, offensive, unity of command, simplicity, and economy of force. They provide a mental framework to address problems in warfare.
8. *Merriam-Webster Online Dictionary,* http://www.m-w.com/.

9. U.S. Constitution, art. 2, sec. 2 (from http://www.archives.gov/national-archives-experience/charters/constitution_transcript.html), states:

The President shall be Commander in Chief of the Army and Navy of the United States, and of the Militia of the several States, when called into the actual Service of the United States; he may require the Opinion, in writing, of the principal Officer in each of the executive Departments, upon any Subject relating to the Duties of their respective Offices, and he shall have Power to grant Reprieves and Pardons for Offences against the United States, except in Cases of Impeachment. He shall have Power, by and with the Advice and Consent of the Senate, to make Treaties, provided two thirds of the Senators present concur; and he shall nominate, and by and with the Advice and Consent of the Senate, shall appoint Ambassadors, other public Ministers and Consuls, Judges of the supreme Court, and all other Officers of the United States, whose Appointments are not herein otherwise provided for, and which shall be established by Law: but the Congress may by Law vest the Appointment of such inferior Officers, as they think proper, in the President alone, in the Courts of Law, or in the Heads of Departments.

10. U.S. Constitution, art. 1, sec. 8 (from http://www.archives.gov/national-archives-experience/charters/constitution_transcript.html) states:

The Congress shall have Power To lay and collect Taxes, Duties, Imposts and Excises, to pay the Debts and provide for the common Defence and general Welfare of the United States; but all Duties, Imposts and Excises shall be uniform throughout the United States; . . . to define and punish Piracies and Felonies committed on the high Seas, and Offences against the Law of Nations; to declare War, grant Letters of Marque and Reprisal, and make Rules concerning Captures on Land and Water; to raise and support Armies, but no Appropriation of Money to that Use shall be for a longer Term than two Years; to provide and maintain a Navy; to make Rules for the Government and Regulation of the land and naval Forces; to provide for calling forth the Militia to execute the Laws of the Union, suppress Insurrections and repel Invasions; to provide for organizing, arming, and disciplining, the Militia, and for governing such Part of them as may be employed in the Service of the United States, reserving to the States respectively, the Appointment of the Officers, and the Authority of training the Militia according to the discipline prescribed by Congress; to exercise exclusive Legislation in all Cases whatsoever, over such District (not exceeding ten Miles square) as may, by Cession of particular States, and the Acceptance of Congress, become the Seat of the Government of the United States, and to exercise like Authority over all Places purchased by the Consent of the Legislature of the State in which the Same shall be, for the Erection of Forts, Magazines, Arsenals, dock-Yards, and other needful Buildings; and to make all Laws which shall be necessary and proper for carrying into Execution the foregoing Powers, and all other Powers vested by this Constitution in the Government of the United States, or in any Department or Officer thereof.

11. U.S. Constitution, art. 3, sec. 2 (from http://www.archives.gov/national-archives-experience/charters/constitution_transcript.html) provides that:

    The judicial Power shall extend to all Cases, in Law and Equity, arising under this Constitution, the Laws of the United States, and Treaties made, or which shall be made, under their Authority;—to all Cases affecting Ambassadors, other public Ministers and Consuls;—to all Cases of admiralty and maritime Jurisdiction;—to Controversies to which the United States shall be a Party;—to Controversies between two or more States;—between a State and Citizens of another State;—between Citizens of different States, —between Citizens of the same State claiming Lands under Grants of different States, and between a State, or the Citizens thereof, and foreign States, Citizens or Subjects.

Chapter 4: Leading in the Information Age

1. Endstate refers to the final disposition of an action or a series of actions. It is synonymous with the term outcome.
2. http://www.valourandhorror.com/DB/BACK/Eisenhower_dir.php

3. Harland Cleveland, "Information as Resource," *The Futurist,* December 1982, 34–39.
4. Don Clark, "Knowledge Management," online reference http://www.nwlink.com/~donclark/knowledge/km.html.
5. *ComputerWorld,* January 3, 2000, 28.
6. i2 Limited, *i2's Analyst's Notebook,* online reference http://www.i2.co.uk/Products/Analysts_Notebook/default.asp (accessed August 23, 2005).
7. Visual Analytics, from online reference http://www.visualanalytics.com/Products/VisuaLinks.cfm# fr (accessed August 23, 2005).
8. Malcolm Gladwell, *Blink: The Power of Thinking Without Thinking* (New York: Time Warner Book Group, 2005), inside cover.
9. *Merriam-Webster Online Dictionary,* s.v. "imagination" (http://www.m-w.com/cgi-bin/dictionary?book=Dictionary&va=imagination&x=22&y=15).
10. Frank Tiboni, "DOD's 'Manhattan Project,'" *Federal Computer Week,* August 29, 2005.
11. *Merriam-Webster Online Dictionary,* s.v. "innovation" (http://www.m-w.com/cgi-bin/dictionary?book=Dictionary&va=innovation).
12. Lean Investments, LLC, "Leading the Lean Enterprise Transformation" (briefing, gk@simpler.com, 2000).
13. *Merriam-Webster Online Dictionary,* s.v. "initiative" (http://www.m-w.com/cgi-bin/dictionary?book=Dictionary&va=initiative).
14. Elbert Hubbard, *A Message to Garcia* (White Plains, NY: A Peter Pauper Press Book, 1982).
15. Ibid., 21–23.
16. Ibid., 11.
17. "Strategic Leadership," briefing to Gen. Maxwell Thurman, Army War College, Carlisle, PA, February 11, 1991.

Chapter 5: Three Big Ideas for U.S. National Leadership in the Information Age

1. Deoxyribonucleic acid (DNA), genetic material of all cellular organisms and most viruses. DNA carries the information needed to

direct *protein synthesis* and *replication*. From *Encarta Dictionary,* http://encarta.msn.com/encyclopedia_761561874/Deoxyribonucleic_Acid.html (accessed October 3, 2005).

2. Bill Nichols and Richard Benedetto, "Govs to Bush: Relief Our Job," *USA Today,* October 3, 2005.
3. Jeb Bush, "Think Locally on Relief," *Washington Post,* September 30, 2005.
4. Rick Jervis, "Iraq Rebuilding Slows as U.S. Money for Projects Dries Up," *USA Today,* October 10, 2005.
5. Bradley Graham and Robin Wright, "Aid to Iraq Ministries to Shift to Pentagon," *Washington Post,* September 26, 2005.
6. President John F. Kennedy, inaugural address (Washington, DC, January 20, 1961).
7. Definition of Moore's Law, http://www.webopedia.com/TERM/M/Moores_Law.html (accessed October 7, 2005).
8. Population data from http://esa.un.org/unpp/p2k0data.asp (accessed October 7, 2005) and transportation data from http://www.t21.ca/transport/ (accessed October 7, 2005).
9. *Encyclopedia Britannica Online,* s.v. "League of Nations," http://www.britannica.com/eb/article-9055027 (accessed September 9, 2004).
10. Ibid. Noteworthy successes included settling the Swedish-Finnish dispute over the Aland Islands (1920–21), guaranteeing the security of Albania (1921), rescuing Austria from economic disaster, settling the division of Upper Silesia (1922), and preventing the outbreak of war in the Balkans between Greece and Bulgaria (1925). In addition, the League extended considerable aid to refugees; it helped to suppress white slave and opium traffic; it did pioneering work in surveys of health; it extended financial aid to needy states; and it furthered international cooperation in labor relations and many other fields.
11. Central Intelligence Agency, *World Fact Book,* https://www.cia.gov/cia/publications/factbook/index.html (accessed October 7, 2005).
12. From the World Bank's official website, http://web.worldbank.org/WBSITE/EXTERNAL/EXTABOUTUS/0,,contentMDK:

20040565~menuPK:1696892~pagePK:51123644~piPK:329829~theSitePK:29708,00.html (accessed October 2005).

13. From USAID website, http://www.usaid.gov/about_usaid/primer.html (accessed October 10, 2005).

14. Central American–Dominican Republic Free Trade Agreement (CAFTA-DR), U.S. Department of Commerce, http://ita.doc.gov/cafta/index.asp.

15. Laurie Garrett, "HIV and National Security: Where Are the Links?" *Council on Foreign Relations Special Report* (New York, 2005), 17.

Index

About the Author

Daniel M. Gerstein is a retired Army officer and strategist who has served in a variety of key operational and policy assignments during his twenty-six year Army career. His service has included duty in combat, peace enforcement, and humanitarian operations on four continents. He has also participated in several international negotiations including as a member of the Holbrooke Delegation that negotiated the peace settlement in Bosnia-Herzegovina, and the Conventional Armed Forces in Europe (CFE) negotiations that limited conventional weapons in Europe. In 2004–2005, he served as a Military Fellow on the Council on Foreign Relations. He is the author of numerous publications including *Securing America's Future: National Strategy in the Information Age* (September 2005) by Praeger Security International, Greenwood Press. A veteran of the Gulf War and operations in the Balkans, he holds degrees from the United States Military Academy, Georgia Tech, the Army Command and General Staff College, and the National War College. He resides in Alexandria, VA.